For the love of potatoes!

comfort cooking with an american favorite

by darlene kronschnabel

Published by The Guest Cottage Inc. Woodruff, Wisconsin

ISBN 1-930596-18-9
Published by The Guest Cottage
PO Box 848
Woodruff, WI 54568
800-333-8122
www.theguestcottage.com

Please write or call to request a free catalog of other
publications by The Guest Cottage.

Cover and interior design by
Pritchard Design • Doylestown, PA

Edited and indexed by Rebecca Valentine • Windsor, CO

Printed in the United States of America

Library of Congress Cataloging-in-Publication Data

Kronschnabel, Darlene.
  Comfort cooking with an American favorite / by Darlene Kronschnabel.
      p. cm. -- (Versatile vegetable cookbook series ; 1)
 Includes index.
   ISBN 1-930596-18-9 (pbk.)
  1. Cookery (Potatoes) I. Title. II. Series.
 TX803.P8 K76 2001
 641.6'521--dc21
                                    2002011987

This book is affectionately dedicated to my husband, Jerry, for his encouragement, inspiration, and enthusiasm; for serving as Number One taster and critic; and who, through it all, never met a spud he didn't like.

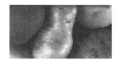

acknowledgments

COLORADO POTATO
ADMINISTRATIVE
COMMITTEE
P.O. Box 348
Monte Vista, Colorado
81144
719-852-3322
www.coloradopotatoes.org

IDAHO POTATO
COMMISSION
P.O. 1068 599 W Bannock
Boise, ID 83701
208 334-2350
www.idahopotato.com

MAINE POTATO BOARD
744 Main Street Suite 1
Presque Isle, ME 04769
207 769-5061
www.mainepotatoes.com

THE NATIONAL POTATO
PROMOTION BOARD
7555 E. Hampden Ave.
#412
Denver, CO 80231
303-369-7783
www.potatohelp.com

THE POTATO
ASSOCIATION OF
AMERICA
University of Maine
5715 Coburn Hall,
Room 6
Orono, ME 04469-5715
Phone: 207-581-3042
Fax: 207-581-3015
E-mail:
umpotato@mail.maine.edu
www.ume.maine.edu/PAA

RED RIVER VALLEY
POTATO GROWERS
ASSOCIATION
420 Business Highway 2
Box 301
East Grand Forks, MN
56721
218 773-3633
www.rrvpotatoes.org

WASHINGTON STATE
POTATO COMMISSION
108 Interlake Road
Moses Lake, WA 98837
509 765-8845
www.potatoes.com

WISCONSIN POTATO &
VEGETABLE GROWERS
ASSOCIATION, INC.
P.O. Box 327
Antigo, WI 54409-0327
715 623-7683
www.potatowis.org

CANADIAN FOOD
INSPECTION AGENCY
www.inspection.gc.ca
www.gc.ca

I want to thank my family and friends who have taste-tested wonderful and not-so-wonderful potato recipes, both in and out of my kitchen, during this past year and still enjoy eating potatoes. Their observations, suggestions and encouragement are greatly appreciated.

A special thanks to the Reference Desk staff at the Pinney Branch of the Madison Public Library for help in researching potato history. Thanks, too, to UW-Extension Nutrition Educator Lori Duchrow at the Oneida County Extension Office, for help in researching potato information.

The versatile potato has a vast resource network in the Potato Growers Associations, who are credited with developing, growing and marketing this nation's number one vegetable. The following have generously offered their help and encouragement in researching and writing this book. For more information or recipes, see resources at right.

Thanks to Frederic Mercure and Janet McDonald of the Potato Section, Plant Health and Production Division, Canadian Food Inspection Agency for their help in locating photo reference for blue potatoes, and for permission to use those photos in this book.

introduction

I'm sure you've heard it said a number of times but it bears repeating: **There are a lot of good things to be said about potatoes.** Perhaps the best is that they are versatile enough to be prepared in a variety of wonderful ways.

Steamed, boiled, broiled, roasted, grilled, baked, sautéed, deep-fried, mashed or microwaved, potatoes are great for a quick snack, a casual family meal, or if you wish, *haute cuisine*. The potato is perfect as an appetizer or snack, in soups and stews, salads, main and side dishes, dumplings, breads, stuffings, desserts—even candy.

The spud has so many great qualities it's hard to select its best. Considering that potatoes are nutritious, tasty, economical, quick and easy to prepare, it's no wonder they're America's favorite vegetable. Depending where you shop—farmers' market, supermarket, or gourmet vegetable market—you'll discover the delectable tuber in a variety of shapes, sizes, textures, and flavors. You may be surprised by the wondrous rainbow of colors: from white to purple, red to pink, yellow to blue. Potatoes blend well with many other ingredients, spices, and herbs to produce tempting dishes to please every taste. No other vegetable is served so often.

The one constant is that, in this age of trendy fast food and instant meals, potatoes have never lost their charm. Like a well-seasoned traveler, the king of vegetables has maintained a lively degree of delicious sophistication. Any way you slice, prepare, or serve the spectacular spud, it lends an earthy yet comforting and homey touch to family meals.

I've gathered 115 sensational potato recipes for your enjoyment. Some offer new ideas; others are traditional. Some are simple; some are sophisticated. None require the skills of a gourmet cook; they only taste that way. Try them all, and decide for yourself which recipe is best.

a brief history of the potato

Consider the humble potato. We tend to take the unspectacular tuber for granted, but how many vegetables can claim to have influenced the course of history?

Most sources agree the potato originated in the Andes of Bolivia and Peru. It was there, in about the mid-1500s, that the Spanish conquistadors discovered the real Inca treasure...the potato!

It is thought Peru's Inca natives first cultivated the potato about 750 BC. Potatoes were an important part of the Inca way of life. The varieties used by the Incas ranged in size from that of a small nut to that of an apple, and in color from red and gold to blue and black.

Potatoes not only served as the Incas' main food and a source to make fermented drink, but as a means to measure time. These native people correlated units of time by how long it took for potatoes to cook. The potato also played a part in healing practices. Raw slices were placed on broken bones, believed to prevent rheumatism. Potatoes were also eaten with other foods to prevent indigestion.

It's not difficult to understand why the Incas felt the potato was a gift bestowed upon them. As such, these simple tubers became objects of pride and worship. The Incas celebrated potato rituals and offered human sacrifices to potato deities.

While these South American Indians referred to their crop as *papas*, the Spanish took to calling them *potata*, a slight variation precursing our modern American term *potato*.

Pleased with their find and appreciative of its food value, the Spaniards returned with the potato to Europe. There it met with suspicion and disdain. For more than a century after its first appearance there, the potato was grown only in flower gardens in England and on the Continent. Most people considered it a botanical curiosity with showy flowers. They regarded it with suspicion because the potato, like the tomato and bell pepper, is a member of the poisonous nightshade family.

Other plants in the nightshade family include: capsicum peppers, ground cherries, eggplant, tobacco, British arrowroot, belladonna, guinea pepper and nicotine. All to some degree contain poisonous alkaloids, which make up the bitter-tasting nitrogen compound produced by plants. Some of these compounds, such as codeine, morphine and quinine, are used for medicinal purposes.

Others, including nicotine and the solanine produced in potatoes that are exposed to light, are poisonous. Wealthy Europeans complained that the potato was unattractive, added no style to their tables, and had no culinary history. How could it be a wholesome food, they questioned, when it was not mentioned in the Bible?

Potatoes first became fashionable when French Queen Marie Antoinette paraded through the countryside wearing potato blossoms in her hair. Cooked potatoes soon became the rage in Parisian Court circles when Marie and her husband, King Louis XVI, served them at the royal table. Soon, top chefs in France and Germany were creating potato dishes at the *haute cuisine* level. It is claimed that Benjamin Franklin attended a French banquet where the fare was nothing but potatoes, prepared twenty different ways.

In the early eighteenth century, Sir Walter Raleigh introduced potatoes to the Irish when he planted them on the Ireland estate given to him by Queen Elizabeth. The Irish poor readily accepted the tuber, recognizing the value of its versatility and ease of cultivation. Even today, white potatoes are often referred to as "Irish" potatoes, in differentiation from sweet potatoes.

In fact, the potato became such a staple in the Irish diet that it replaced almost all other crops. There was a time when it was estimated that Irish adults ate from eight to ten pounds of potatoes a day. This single-crop agricultural dependence nearly wiped out the country when the crop failed due to blight in 1845 and 1846, and spurred the first of the large Western European migrations to America, in search of relief from starvation.

The white potato made it to American shores about 1720. First grown in Londonderry, New Hampshire, it didn't become a serious crop until planted in considerable quantity in Salem, Massachusetts, fifteen years before the Revolution. However, it remained a food of suspicion until the mid-1800s.

Those early Spanish explorers might not recognize today's humble potato. Thanks to scientific development and agricultural skills, our favorite vegetable has more flavor and better resistance to disease. Potatoes are grown in all fifty states, which says a lot about their freshness and availability to consumers.

Today, we serve potatoes in a wide range of deliciously different dishes, from sensational salads to sophisticated classics to crusty pizza and more. The results? Fantastic! Proving that from the poor man's food to the gourmet's delight, the potato can warm everyone's soul.

how to spot a perfect potato

As with all cookery, it is the quality of the basic ingredients that is of primary importance. The same principle holds true as you shop for potatoes. When making your selection, look for potatoes that are:

- clean, firm and relatively smooth. Lumpy potatoes are not bad, but there is greater waste when peeling them.
- uniform in kind and size to provide even cooking.

And avoid those that show any signs of:

- decay, dark spots or cuts.
- wrinkled, wilted skins or sprouting eyes. All indicate improper storage and old potatoes.
- musty or moldy odors that can give an off-flavor to cooked potatoes.
- a greenish cast or tint. Green spots indicate improper handling and storage that exposes the potatoes to light, which causes surface concentrations of a toxic alkaloid called solanine. The flavor of the cooked potato will be bitter, and eating a green potato could make you ill.

the potato test

If you are having trouble deciding which potato is best for baking (starchy) or best for boiling (waxy) here is a simple test from Harold McGee's *On Food and Cooking*: Make a brine of 2 parts water to 1 part salt. Add the potato. If it floats, it's waxy and if it sinks, it's starchy.

buying tips

Take the guesswork out of the amount of potatoes to buy for any particular use by checking the following guide.

Fresh Potatoes

- 1 pound of potatoes equals:
- about 3 medium potatoes
- 3 cups peeled and sliced
- 2½ cups peeled and diced
- 2 cups mashed
- 2 cups French fries

Potato Salad

2 pounds medium potatoes equals about 6 servings of potato salad or one potato per serving.

storage tips

- Potatoes store very well in a cool, dry, dark place that is well ventilated. A kitchen closet works quite well, as does a dry basement. Avoid storing them under the kitchen sink (it may be too damp).

- Remove the plastic bag the potatoes come in at once and place the loose potatoes in a vegetable bin, open container, or net bag to allow free air circulation.

- Never wash potatoes before storage, as this speeds the development of decay.

- At ideal temperatures (45° to 50°F), potatoes will keep well for several weeks. If stored at room temperature, potatoes should be used within a week.

- Temperatures over 50°F encourage sprouting and shriveling. You can still use sprouting potatoes by breaking off or cutting out the sprouts. There is more waste to the potato at this stage, as they may need to be peeled.

- Potatoes should not be refrigerated. At temperatures below 40°F, potatoes develop a sweet taste, a result of some of the potato's starch turning to sugar. This increase in sugar also causes the potato to become mushy and often discolored when cooked.

- Avoid prolonged exposure of potatoes to either sunlight or overhead lighting fixtures, which will cause them to turn green. This greening produces a bitter flavor. If a small amount of greening does occur, pare away the affected area before the potato is used.

- Avoid storing them under the kitchen sink (it may be too damp).

the nutritional value of potatoes

There is more to a potato than meets the eye. Where else can you find such a perfect combination of nutrition and taste? It's hard to believe there can be so much goodness in such a modest vegetable.

For starters, potatoes are low in calories, with only about 110 per medium-size potato (about 3 potatoes per pound).

In addition, the power-packed tuber is an excellent source of many nutrients. Consider the following characteristics of the potato:

• Like an orange, high in Vitamin C
• Good source of Vitamin B-6, which aids in the metabolism of protein, fats, and carbohydrates
• High in fiber
• No fat, no cholesterol
• Low in sodium
• More potassium than a banana
• More useable iron than any other vegetable
• Chock full of complex carbohydrates
• Protein in potatoes is among the best to be found in vegetables. In fact, if you ate nothing more than one potato every day, you'd meet your daily protein intake requirements.

basic potato cookery

Don't let anyone tell you the potato is ordinary. Boiled, baked or fried, hot or cold, plain or fancy, potatoes are our most popular and versatile vegetable. They can be served from breakfast through dinner, for special parties or as snacks throughout the day. Whether you're cooking for company or for your family, great potato recipes start with one of the following basic cooking techniques.

preparation tips

• Gently wash and scrub potatoes under cold running water, with a vegetable brush or cellulose sponge.

• Cook potatoes in their skins whenever possible to preserve nutrients. If you must peel them first, use a vegetable peeler to keep peelings as thin as possible since many of the potato's nutrients are found close to the skin.

• Cooking times may vary according to the type and variety of potato and how long the potato has been stored after being harvested.

To bake: Before baking, pierce the skin of each potato several times with the tines of a fork to allow steam to escape, which prevents bursting during cooking. Do not spoil the texture of potatoes by wrapping them in foil before baking. This steams rather then bakes the potato. A medium potato, placed directly on the oven rack, bakes in 40 to 45 minutes at 400° or you can bake at temperatures 325° to 400° with whatever you have in the oven. Adjust baking times according to oven temperatures. Potatoes are done when they are soft when squeezed with a mitted hand or pierced with a fork. Use a fork to gently open the potato and fluff up the delicious white solids inside.

To boil: Don't drown potatoes in water. Use as little as possible—about an inch—to prevent nutrient loss. In a heavy saucepan with a tight-fitting lid, cook the potatoes in boiling salted water until fork tender. Whole potatoes take 30 to 40 minutes; sliced, chopped, or diced, 20 to 25 minutes. Watch closely.

If water cooks away, add more.

To steam: Place a perforated rack in the bottom of a heavy saucepan. Add water to just below the rack, about ½ inch. Heat water to boiling. Arrange potatoes on the rack. Cover with a tight-fitting lid and cook until fork tender. Whole, 30 to 45 minutes; cut-up, 20 to 30 minutes. Check water level occasionally to make sure water does not boil away.

To pan roast: Arrange peeled, raw halved or quartered potatoes around meat in roasting pan about 1 to 1½ hours (depending on potato size) before serving. Baste occasionally with meat drippings. Turn frequently to brown. Roast until fork tender.

To microwave: For best results using a microwave oven, select low moisture, uniform-sized potatoes. Wash, but do not dry. Pierce each potato in several places with the tines of a fork. Place potatoes about 1 inch apart, spoke-fashion, on a double layer of paper toweling with the small ends toward the center. As each microwave is different, check your manual for directions. Potato size and variety may vary the cooking times. Cook a medium to large potato on high an average of 4 minutes. Add 1 to 2 minutes cooking time for each potato. Turn potatoes over about halfway through cooking. After removing from the microwave, let stand; the potato will continue to cook for about 5 minutes.

To french fry: Peel and cut large potatoes into strips about ¼ to ½ inch thick. If using small potatoes, cut into quarters.

Toss cut-up potatoes into a bowl of ice water to keep crisp and white. Heat four inches of vegetable oil to 390° in a deep fat fryer or large heavy saucepan. Blot potatoes dry with paper towels. Place a layer of potatoes (do not crowd) in a wire basket. Immerse the whole basket in hot oil or with long-handled tongs, place a few at a time directly into the oil. Cook about 5 minutes or until golden brown and tender. Drain on paper towels. Sprinkle lightly with salt and serve at once.

To oven fry: Peel and cut potatoes as you would for French fries. As potatoes are sliced, toss into cold water to keep white. Preheat oven to 500°. Drain potatoes and pat dry. Toss in a bowl with one to two tablespoons of vegetable oil until all potatoes are lightly coated. Spread in a single layer on a baking sheet. Bake until golden on underside, about 15 minutes. Turn strips and bake 5 minutes more or until crisp and golden. Sprinkle lightly with salt and serve immediately.

To pan fry: Thinly slice two to three medium potatoes. Heat one to two tablespoons of oil in a heavy, wide skillet over moderately high heat. Place a single layer of potatoes in skillet. Fry on one side for four minutes, depending on size, until golden brown. Flip and fry on other side until fork tender. Season with salt and pepper. Serve immediately.

how many different ways can you serve potatoes?

Potatoes are as versatile as the alphabet is long. Here are some hints to help you recall old favorites.

- **A is for Almondine**—slivered, blanched almonds, browned in butter, sprinkled over hot mashed potatoes.

- **B is for potato Bread**—including rolls, muffins, biscuits and scones—all old-fashioned favorites made with mashed potatoes.

- **C is for Chips**—America's favorite snack food that is simply very thin potato slices, plain or ridged, flavored or not, fried crisp and salted.

- **D is for Delmonico**—diced potatoes and eggs in a white sauce, topped with buttered crumbs and baked in a casserole.

- **E is for Easy scalloped potatoes**—a classic family recipe that can be varied by using diced ham, sliced Polish sausage, or shredded Cheddar cheese mixed with broccoli florets, sliced carrots, or peas.

- **F is for Fried**—Country fried, French fried, American fried, cottage fried...you take it from there.

- **G is for Grated**—fresh potatoes in potato pancakes.

- **H is for Hash browns**—everyone's favorite.

- **I is for Irish potato dumplings**—potatoes uncooked and grated, or boiled and riced, in these fluffy dumplings.

- **J is for Julienne strips**—perfect for Jansson's Temptation, or simple potato sticks.

- **K is for Kid pleaser**—hot dogs, split lengthwise and stuffed with mashed potatoes, topped with a splash of catsup and sprinkled with shredded Cheddar cheese. Cook in the microwave 1 to 2 minutes or until cheese is melted.

- **L is for Lyonnaise**—potatoes layered with onions, dotted with butter, sprinkled with grated Cheddar or Parmesan cheese, and sautéed.

- **M is for Mashed potatoes**—perhaps with nonfat cream cheese and chives, or horseradish instead of milk and butter.

- **N is for New potatoes**—a special treat when gently boiled with peas, buttered, and coated with parsley.

- **O is for Omelet**—butter or olive oil fried, diced, cooked potatoes with crumbled cooked bacon, minced onion, and your favorite shredded cheese tucked into the omelet fold.

- **P is for Potato skins**—baked or broiled until very crisp, served as a snack or with a meal.

- **Q is for Quick potato products**—the amazing variety of these fresh-tasting packaged potatoes on your market's shelves and in the freezer section are ideal for a busy day.

- **R is for Roasted**—peel and cut into even-sized pieces, place in the roasting pan with meat drippings, and roast 1 to 1½ hours or until done.

- **S is for Stuffed**—another style with loads of variations, served with your choice of toppings.

- **T is for Twice-baked**—great to make ahead with a variety of fillings, from cottage cheese and fresh herbs to minced smoked salmon.

- **U is for Ultimate potato salads**—too numerous to mention, and everyone has their personal favorite.

- **V is for Vichyssoise**—a rich cream of potato and leek or onion soup, served hot or icy cold.

- **W is for Wedges**—raw potatoes dipped in olive oil, coated with spiced crumbs and baked until tender.

- **XYZ is for the exciting assortment** you'll find once you start enjoying the versatile potato.

table of contents

table of contents (cont.)

soups

overview

Homemade soups are the ultimate in comfort food, and this is especially true of potato soups. The potatoes play an important role in soups by binding, enriching and thickening. Best of all, they impart a delightful flavor and texture no other vegetable can match.

It is claimed potato soup originated with the American scientist, Benjamin Thompson, in 1795. According to one source, he wanted to feed the poor "as well as possible with as little as possible." No doubt he didn't realize his innovative recipe's lasting quality—potatoes have been used in soups ever since.

Today, potato soups are quite simple to prepare from scratch, as there are no long hours of simmering, stewing, or pot watching. In most cases, you can do as I've done here by combining leftover mashed potatoes, zesty seasonings, and commercial bouillon cubes or powdered soup bases to make the broth. Add some fresh or frozen vegetables and fresh herbs, and you're off to a good start. Keep in mind, potatoes enjoy the company of chives, paprika or dill, as these lend a delicious flavor to potato soup.

Whatever spice or herb combination you decide to add to your soup, start slow with small amounts, and taste often so that you end up with a flavor you, your family, and guests will enjoy.

The soups I've presented here range from hearty full-meal soups to lighter, first course ones. Some are peasantry favorites, and some have a gourmet flair to them. Sometimes the soup stands alone. Others are topped with a dollop of sour cream, a sprinkle of shredded cheese, chopped green onions or minced chives.

Which soup to make? Don't try to decide when you're hungry...they all seem irresistible!

If a soup or stew is too salty, add a few slices of uncooked potatoes to absorb the excess salt.

potato-spinach bisque

Delicate and elegant, this soup is perfect served as a first course for dinner or as a light lunch all by itself.

4 cups chicken broth
2 cups (well packed) fresh spinach, washed, stemmed, and chopped
6 green onions with tops, thinly sliced
2½ cups mashed potatoes
2 cups half-and-half
½ teaspoon dried oregano
½ teaspoon hot sauce
½ teaspoon freshly ground black pepper
Sour cream, for garnish (optional)
Snipped chives, for garnish (optional)

In a large kettle, bring broth to a boil over medium-high heat. Reduce heat. Stir in the spinach and onions. Cover and simmer for 4 to 5 minutes or until spinach is wilted and onions are tender. Remove from heat. Pour a small portion of the mixture into blender and process until smooth. Repeat with remaining mixture. Return to kettle. Whisk in mashed potatoes, stirring until mixture is smooth.

Blend in half-and-half, oregano, hot sauce, and pepper. Cook over low heat until soup is thoroughly heated. Garnish each serving with a dollop of sour cream and a sprinkle of chives, if desired.

Makes about 6 servings.

chilled potato and beet soup

A colorful, cold soup, perfect for a light luncheon.

2 cups mashed potatoes
2 cups cooked, chopped beets
1 cup minced green onions
3 tablespoons prepared horseradish
½ teaspoon salt
⅛ teaspoon freshly ground black pepper
3 tablespoons lemon juice
2½ cups chicken broth
½ cup sour cream, for garnish (optional)
2 tablespoons snipped fresh dill, for garnish (optional)

In a food processor or blender, combine potatoes, beets, onions, horseradish, salt, pepper, and lemon juice. Cover and process at high speed until very smooth. With processor on add 2 cups of broth. Taste and correct seasoning. Stir in remaining broth. Chill.

Just before serving, add a dollop of sour cream and a sprinkle of snipped dillweed.

Makes about 8 servings.

potato and carrot soup

The flavor and texture of this soup is smooth and creamy. It provides a nice first course for a special meal.

3 tablespoons butter
1 pound carrots, thinly sliced
2 large potatoes, diced
2 sticks celery, diced
1 large onion, diced
3 cups beef broth
1 bay leaf
⅔ cup orange juice
2 tablespoons grated orange rind
1 tablespoon lemon juice
½ teaspoon salt
⅛ teaspoon pepper
1 cup light cream
Orange slices (optional)
Parsley (optional)

In a large saucepan, melt butter over moderate heat. Add carrots, potatoes, celery, and onion; sauté for 8 to 10 minutes, stirring occasionally. Do not brown. Add broth, bay leaf, orange juice, orange rind, lemon juice, salt and pepper. Bring to a boil. Cover and reduce heat to simmer for 25 to 30 minutes. Remove bay leaf. Pour a small portion of the mixture into a food processor or blender and process until smooth. Repeat with remaining mixture. Return to saucepan. Whisk in the cream and adjust seasoning to taste. Heat through. If desired, garnish with orange slices and parsley.

Makes about 6 servings.

quick potato frankfurter soup

Here is a quick and simple soup that is sure to be a kid pleaser. With a dash of imagination, it makes a satisfying lunch.

2 tablespoons butter
1 small onion, chopped
3 large potatoes, peeled and diced
3 tablespoons minced green pepper
1 tablespoon minced sweet red pepper
2 cups chicken broth
½ teaspoon salt
2 cups milk
6 frankfurters, cut in ¼-inch slices
Shredded Cheddar cheese, for garnish

In a large saucepan, melt butter. Add onion and cook until golden. Stir in potatoes and peppers. Add chicken broth and salt. Bring to boiling. Reduce heat and simmer for 35 minutes or until potatoes are tender. Stir in milk and frankfurter slices. Simmer for 3 to 5 minutes longer or until milk and frankfurter slices are heated. Spoon Cheddar cheese over individual portions.

Makes about 6 servings.

Variations

- You may use salami or other luncheon meat, cut in pieces, instead of frankfurters. Allow one slice per person. Or sprinkle the soup with chopped cooked ham before serving.

- For an interesting spicy bite, substitute Pepper Jack cheese for the garnish.

- This soup welcomes extra vegetables such as a ½ cup frozen or canned peas, or ½ cup cooked carrots.

Add about ¾ cup shredded cheese to a quart or more of potato soup before serving. Keep the soup hot and stir just long enough to melt the cheese. To keep cheese from disappearing into the broth, do not boil.

green onion potato soup with spaetzle

For a light supper, serve with crusty bread and a green salad.

1½ cups sliced green onions, tops included
1 clove garlic, minced
1 tablespoon olive oil
5 cups chicken broth
1 cup milk
2 cups mashed potatoes
1 medium carrot, shredded
1½ cups spaetzle*
Freshly ground black pepper, to taste
Parsley, snipped for garnish

In a medium saucepan, over medium heat, sauté onions and garlic in oil, stirring occasionally, until onions are wilted, but not browned. Add broth. Bring to a boil. Remove from heat and stir in milk, potatoes, carrots and spaetzle. Return to heat and cook for 5 minutes longer or until thoroughly heated. Season with pepper. Sprinkle with parsley.

Makes about 6 servings.

**spaetzle

Spaetzle arrived in the Midwest with German immigrants. The delicate, light egg dumplings are popular in Germany and Austria today where they are sometimes served warm—Heaven forbid—in place of potatoes. However, they go quite well with all kinds of soup, especially with Green Onion Potato. Why not try your hand at making your own? Here's the recipe.

2 cups all-purpose flour
1 teaspoon salt
⅛ teaspoon pepper
2 eggs
⅔ cup milk
1 tablespoon of water or more, if needed

In a small bowl combine flour, salt, and pepper. In a deep mixing bowl beat eggs until foamy. Mix in milk. Slowly add the flour to the egg mixture, a little at a time, beating by hand until the batter is smooth. If the batter is too stiff to go through the holes of a colander or spaetzle maker, add water, 1 tablespoon at a time. Bring a large pot filled with water to a rolling boil over medium-high heat. Spoon a few tablespoonfuls of batter into a large-holed colander or spaetzle maker. Holding it over the boiling water, press the batter quickly through the holes, dropping the spaetzle into the boiling water.** Prepare only as many as will fit in the width of the kettle. Cook spaetzle uncovered for 2 to 3 minutes. Spaetzle will rise to surface when done. Remove spaetzle with a slotted spoon, and drain. Repeat with remaining batter. They should have a soft, dough-like texture. Serve warm, tossed with melted butter and parsley, or in soup.

Makes about 6 servings.

**Note
You need to work very fast when you're pushing the batter through the holes, as the steam from the boiling water underneath will cook the spaetzle and plug the holes of the utensil.

potato and cabbage soup

This is a hearty potato soup. With plenty of beef and bacon, it makes a whole meal when served with a salad.

1½ pounds lean beef,
   cut into 1-inch cubes
2 tablespoons vegetable or olive oil
4 cups beef broth
4 cups coarsely shredded cabbage (divided)
1 cup chopped onion
¼ pound bacon, chopped
1 large garlic clove, minced
2 teaspoons salt
½ teaspoon pepper
½ teaspoon dry mustard
3 cups water
2 large potatoes, peeled and cubed
   (about 4 cups)
2 large sweet potatoes, peeled and cubed
   (about 4 cups)
3 tablespoons tomato paste

In a large kettle or Dutch oven, brown beef in oil. Add broth, 2 cups cabbage, onion, bacon, garlic, salt, pepper, and dry mustard. Bring to a boil. Reduce heat and simmer, partially covered, for 1 hour. Add water, potatoes, tomato paste and remaining 2 cups cabbage. Cover and simmer for 1 hour or until potatoes are fork tender. Taste to adjust seasoning.

Makes about 5 quarts.

country style potato leek soup

This soup is deceptively delicate in appearance, but robust enough to satisfy just about any appetite.

4 large leeks
2 tablespoons butter
2 medium onions, chopped (2 cups)
5 medium russet potatoes,
   peeled and cubed (5 cups)
5 cups chicken broth
1 bay leaf
½ teaspoon salt
3 to 4 drops hot pepper sauce (to taste)
⅛ teaspoon garlic powder
Various optional garnishes:
   chopped fresh parsley, dried parsley,
   snipped fresh dill, crisply cooked and
   crumbled bacon, shredded Cheddar
   cheese, or a sprinkle of paprika

Wash leeks thoroughly under cold running water. Shred into thin slices, including part of green tops. In a large saucepan over medium high heat, melt butter. Add leeks and onions. Cook, stirring occasionally, for 6 to 8 minutes or until golden, but not brown. Stir in potatoes, broth and bay leaf. Bring to a boil. Reduce heat. Cover and simmer for 20 to 30 minutes or until potatoes are tender. Remove from heat. In a blender, food processor, or food mill, purée the soup until smooth. Return to the saucepan. Stir in salt, hot pepper sauce and garlic powder. Cook for 5 minutes more or until heated through. Do not boil. Ladle soup into bowl and garnish to your liking. Serve immediately.

Makes about 6 servings.

Potato soup can be stored in a freezer for up to 3 months. Chill soup, then pour into a freezer container, leaving 1-inch head space per quart—food expands when frozen.

hungarian
potato-mushroom soup

Hungarians enjoy the savory influence of paprika, even in soup. This recipe makes an enticing, rich soup, satisfying and delicious in the best Hungarian tradition. If the amount of paprika startles you, simply adjust the amount to your taste.

2 tablespoons butter
1 medium onion, chopped
1 pound mushrooms, sliced
1 green pepper, finely chopped
1 carrot, diced
4 rounded teaspoons sweet paprika
2 tablespoons all-purpose flour
3 medium potatoes, peeled and diced
   (to make 4 cups)
6 cups chicken broth
2 teaspoons snipped fresh dillweed
   OR ¾ teaspoon dried dillweed
⅓ cup chopped fresh parsley and extra
   for optional garnish
2 bay leaves
1 cup sour cream
Salt and pepper, to taste

In a large kettle over medium-high heat, melt the butter. Add onion, mushrooms, green pepper, carrot, and paprika. Sauté and stir until vegetables are tender. Lower the heat and stir in the flour. Continue cooking for 2 to 3 minutes. Add the potatoes, broth, dill, bay leaves and parsley and continue cooking over high heat until the broth comes to a boil. Lower heat, partially cover, and simmer gently for 30 to 40 minutes or until the potatoes are fork tender. Remove from heat. Remove bay leaves. Blend in the sour cream until well blended. Season with salt and pepper to taste. Serve hot, either plain or with a sprinkle of fresh chopped parsley.

Makes 4 to 6 servings.

cheesy corn
and potato chowder

A tasty but quick and simple chowder for those days when kitchen time is short.

2 tablespoons butter or margarine
1 cup chopped onions
½ cup chopped celery
1 pound red potatoes, cooked, peeled,
   and diced (about 3 cups)
2 cups milk
1 can (15 ounces) cream style corn
½ teaspoon salt
⅛ teaspoon pepper
2 cups (8 ounces) shredded Cheddar cheese
Snipped parsley, for garnish (optional)

In a large saucepan, melt butter. Sauté onion and celery until tender, for about 10 minutes. Add potatoes, milk and corn, salt and pepper. Cook over medium heat for 12 to 15 minutes or until potatoes are tender and all ingredients reach serving temperature. Remove from heat and stir in cheese until melted. If necessary, return to low to finish melting cheese. Do not boil. Serve warm, garnished with chopped parsley if desired.

Makes about 6 servings.

manhattan clam and potato chowder

The addition of tomatoes with the clams has caused this to be called the "red" clam chowder.

¼ cup butter
1 onion, diced (1 cup)
2 medium red potatoes, diced (1½ cups)
1 cup diced celery
¾ cup diced carrots
¼ cup diced green pepper
1 can (28 ounces) whole tomatoes, drained, chopped
1 cup water
1 teaspoon dried leaf thyme
2 cans (6½ ounces each) minced clams, undrained
Salt and pepper to taste
Snipped parsley, for garnish

In a large saucepan, melt butter. Add onions and cook until lightly browned. Add potatoes, celery, carrots, green pepper, tomatoes, water, and thyme. Add extra water if needed to cover vegetables. Bring to a boil. Reduce heat to simmer, covered, for 35 to 40 minutes or until vegetables are tender. Stir in clams. Cook and stir for 3 to 4 minutes more to allow clams to heat thoroughly. Season to taste. Serve warm with a sprinkle of chopped parsley.

Makes about 6 servings.

salmon potato chowder

This chowder has a rich flavor. If you wish, serve it with a light salad and a basket of whole grain bread and crackers.

2 tablespoons butter or margarine
2 cups peeled and diced red potatoes
1 cup diced carrots
½ cup chopped onion
½ cup chopped celery
½ cup chopped green pepper
1 can (14.5 ounces) diced tomatoes
2 cups chicken broth
½ teaspoon salt
⅛ teaspoon pepper
⅛ teaspoon dried crushed thyme
3 cups milk, divided
1 can (14.75 ounces) salmon, drained, boned and flaked
3 tablespoons flour
Snipped chives, for garnish (optional)

In a large kettle or Dutch oven, melt the butter. Add potatoes, carrots, onion, celery, and green pepper. Sauté, stirring often, for about 5 minutes. Add tomatoes, broth, salt, pepper, and thyme. Cover and simmer for 8 to 10 minutes. Stir in 2½ cups milk and salmon. Simmer, covered, for 20 to 25 minutes or until vegetables are tender. Combine remaining ½ cup milk and flour, stirring until smooth. Blend into chowder and simmer, stirring often, uncovered, until slightly thickened. Ladle into deep bowls and garnish with minced chives if desired.

Makes about 1½ quarts.

Some seasonings will intensify with freezing and some will lose their strength—it's a good idea to leave seasoning adjustments until after thawing.

polish potato and sausage soup

The sausage flavor is hearty and pleasing, the texture rich and warming. It makes this soup perfect for a whole meal when served with a salad and crusty bread.

2 tablespoons butter or margarine
1 pound Kielbasa cut into ¼-inch slices
2 cups chopped celery and leaves
1 cup chopped onion
4 cups shredded cabbage
2 cups thinly sliced carrots
1½ cups beef broth
5 cups of water
2 tablespoons cider vinegar
1 tablespoon salt
1 bay leaf
½ teaspoon dried leaf thyme
3 cups peeled and cubed red potatoes
Pepper, to taste

In a large kettle or Dutch oven, melt butter. Add kielbasa, celery, and onion. Cook over medium-low heat for about 5 minutes or until celery and onion are wilted, but not browned. Add cabbage, carrots, broth, water, vinegar, salt, bay leaf, and thyme. Bring to a boil; reduce heat. Cover and simmer for 1½ hours. Add potatoes, cover and cook for 25 minutes longer or until potatoes are tender. Season with pepper to taste.

Makes about 8 servings.

Note
Kielbasa is sometimes referred to as Polish Sausage. It is highly flavored, lightly smoked, coarsely chopped pork with some beef and veal, mixed spices and loose garlic sausage meat. Any similarly flavored sausage may be substituted for kielbasa.

salads

overview

The potato is at its versatile best in salads. What's best is that you can serve potato salads often and not repeat the same recipe.

seasonings

Condiments, spices and other flavorings can help you be creative and personalize your potato salads. Best of all, they add flavor and a gourmet touch.

Use the following suggestions with discrimination, and not all in one salad: Your favorite flavored, prepared, coarse-ground Dijon or sweet-hot mustard; wine vinegars such as balsamic, raspberry, red or white; olive oil, freshly squeezed lime or lemon juice; pickle relish, pickle juice, capers, or caraway seeds; celery salt, celery seeds, rosemary, or tarragon; minced garlic or garlic powder; dill, snipped fresh or dried; paprika; hot pepper sauce (only a few drops); curry powder, and horseradish.

garnishes

Yes, it's true. Potato salads, with all their usual variety, will be more tempting if you give them a little special decoration. The basic purpose of your garnish is to lend eye appeal to your potato salad. In effect, it is the finishing touch, so be sure to make it just as good to see as it is to eat.

Above all, even when decorated, keep it simple. Sometimes all you need is a ruffle of lettuce, a sprinkling of colorful shredded carrots, or rings of green and red peppers. You might even add a touch of radish slices, diced celery, crisp croutons, strips of pimiento, tomato wedges, cauliflower or broccoli florets.

You can also dress it up with cucumber slices, shreds of red cabbage, snipped fresh parsley or dill, watercress sprigs, coarsely chopped walnuts, hard-cooked egg slices or wedges, apple wedges, or crisp bacon bits.

- Dress up prepared potato salads with plumped dried tomato halves and snipped fresh parsley.

- Arrange thin tomato wedges, skin-side up, in a flower petal design with either alfalfa sprouts, sprigs of parsley, or watercress for leaves.

- Surround a lettuce-lined platter of potato salad with an assortment of pretty salad trimmings such as:

  - **Cucumber Accordion** Cut a 3-inch length of split peeled cucumber, slice thin almost to the flat side. Poke thin radish slices in cuts.

  - **Onion Ruffle** Trim root from a green onion, then shred the top about three inches. Place in a bowl of ice and water to curl.

  - **Carrot Curls** Slice the length of scraped raw carrots paper-thin with a peeler. Crisp in ice water until curled.

  - **Celery Flute** Slit 2-inch lengths of celery into narrow strips, cutting from ends toward the middle. Chill until strips curl slightly.

  - **Radish Pompon** Slice a trimmed radish one way, then crosswise, almost through to the stem. Chill in ice water until opened into a puffy, flowerlike ball.

  - **Pickle Fan** Slice small pickles into 5 or 6 strips, starting at the tip end and cutting almost to stem. Spread slices to form open fans.

"a word to the wise"
To Make And Keep Potato Salads Even More Enjoyable

• To avoid the risk of food poisoning, never leave potato salad at room temperature for more than two hours, including preparation time. After mixing the salad, put it in shallow containers to remove the heat produced in preparation and to allow more rapid chilling, then refrigerate and chill thoroughly.

• Of course, if you are making hot potato salad, then you'll need to keep it hot.

• If you have any doubts, remember to:
Keep cold potato salad cold.
Keep hot potato salad hot.

• For picnics, cookouts and potlucks, keep cold potato salads on ice or use small dishes and replenish from the refrigerator. For hot salads, use a heating dish or reheat small servings from the refrigerator and replenish the serving dishes.

• Promptly refrigerate potato salad after meals; don't let it sit on the table or counter. Divide leftovers into small containers for quick cooling in the refrigerator.

• Potato salad will keep in the refrigerator for 2 to 3 days. After that, it loses quality and may become watery.

tips for potato salads

• You may interchange the kinds of potatoes used in salads. I prefer a dry, mealy potato in some salads, while in others I believe new or red potatoes make a terrific choice. My suggestion to you is to experiment and go with your preference.

• It's best not to peel potatoes when cooking for salad. Cooking potatoes in their "jackets" will not only save nutrients, it will help them hold their shapes.

However, to make potato salad more quickly, cook the potatoes already peeled and diced.

• If you're going to cook your potatoes whole, choose ones of similar size, so they will all finish cooking at about the same time.

• Take care not to overcook mealy potatoes, like russets. Drain them as soon as you can pierce them easily with a fork.

• Don't cut ingredients too small or the final salad will be mushy, with no textural interest.

• To keep the bite-size pieces intact, use a rubber spatula to gently turn the potatoes while mixing with the dressing.

• To ensure a deep-down flavor, peel potatoes while steaming hot, cut them, sprinkle them with vinegar, white wine, or an oil and vinegar dressing. Hot potatoes absorb flavors as they cool. Cold potatoes will not.

• The French serve potato salad at room temperature, but dress it while it's hot, as the Germans do, so that the potatoes readily absorb the good flavors in the dressing.

• For potato salad with a snap, toss peeled boiled potatoes with prepared bottled dressings such as French, ranch, or Bleu cheese, then garnish with chopped green onions.

• Add leftover diced, cooked chicken or turkey, cubed ham or strips of grilled steak or roast beef for a main-dish potato salad.

• Add a little mustard (dry or prepared) to the mayonnaise you put in potato salad.

• Potato salad tastes best if prepared ahead and chilled overnight to allow the flavors to blend.

• Don't make hasty judgments on the seasonings. Let the salad stand overnight before adding more of anything.

spicy pineapple and shrimp potato salad

The mixture of flavors, colors, and textures, combined with the spicy pineapple dressing, make this a delicious side or main dish salad. Serve with banana or blueberry muffins.

6 medium unpeeled red potatoes, about 2 pounds
1 12-ounce package frozen, peeled, cooked shrimp
1 cup chopped zucchini
1½ cups spiced pineapple*
½ cup sliced green onions
⅓ cup chopped red bell pepper
⅓ cup chopped celery
½ cup mayonnaise or salad dressing
½ cup spiced pineapple juice*
¼ cup extra virgin olive oil
2 tablespoons lime juice
1 teaspoon salt
1/2 teaspoon hot pepper sauce
Spinach or romaine lettuce leaves
1 lemon, sliced for garnish
1 lime, sliced for garnish

In a large saucepan, cook potatoes, covered, in lightly salted boiling water for about 20 to 25 minutes or until tender. Drain. Cool slightly. Peel and cube. In a large bowl, combine potatoes, shrimp, zucchini, spiced pineapple, onions, pepper, and celery. Toss lightly to mix. For dressing, in a small bowl whisk together mayonnaise, spiced pineapple juice, olive oil, lime juice, salt and hot pepper sauce. Add dressing to salad mixture. Toss gently to coat. Cover and chill several hours or overnight to allow flavors to blend. Serve salad on a spinach or romaine leaf lined platter or individual salad plates garnished with twisted lemon and lime slices.

Makes about 8 main dish servings.

*spicy pineapple and juice

1 20-ounce can pineapple chunks (juice packed)
½ cup white wine vinegar
¼ cup sugar
12 coriander seeds
8 whole cloves
1 teaspoon mustard seeds
½ inch fresh ginger

Drain pineapple chunks, reserving juice. Set aside. In a small saucepan, combine ½ cup pineapple juice, sugar, white wine vinegar, coriander seeds, cloves, mustard seeds and ginger. Bring to a boil over medium heat and simmer for 5 minutes. Add pineapple chunks and simmer for 6 to 8 minutes. Drain, reserving spiced pineapple juice. Discard coriander seeds, cloves and ginger. Cool before using.

Makes about 2 cups.

Early Potato Salad: John Gerrard in 1597 writes about potatoes and their virtues and said that "they are sometimes boiled and sopped in wine, by others boiled with prunes, and likewise others dress them (after roasting them in the ashes) in oil, vinegar and salt, every man according to his own taste. However they be dressed, they comfort, nourish and strengthen the body." – Arnold Shircliffe, sharing one of the first mentions of potato salad found in any book.

From *The Edgewater Beach Hotel Salad* book, 1926

warm oriental potato salad

This Oriental-inspired salad can easily be prepared to make any cookout memorable. Enhanced with crisp vegetables, water chestnuts, cashews, and pungent sesame-soy dressing, the salad complements sweet-n-sour barbecued chicken or pork.

3 tablespoons salad oil
4 medium potatoes, halved lengthwise
   and thinly sliced (about 1½ pounds)
1 cup carrots, thinly sliced on the diagonal
1 cup celery, thinly sliced on the diagonal
½ cup green sweet pepper
   cut in julienne strips
½ cup red sweet pepper
   cut in julienne strips
½ cup sliced mushrooms
½ cup sliced water chestnuts
½ cup unsalted dry roasted cashews
1 clove garlic, minced
1 teaspoon grated ginger root
½ cup water
2 tablespoons light soy sauce
1 teaspoon toasted sesame oil
1½ teaspoons cornstarch
1 large tomato, cut in thin wedges
⅓ cup sliced green onions

In a large nonstick skillet, heat 1½ tablespoons of the oil over medium-high heat. Add the potatoes. Cook and stir for about 10 minutes or until barely tender. Remove the potatoes and keep warm. Add the remaining oil to the skillet, followed by the carrots, celery, peppers, mushrooms, water chestnuts, cashews, garlic, and grated ginger root. Cook and stir over medium-high heat for 3 to 4 minutes or until vegetables are crisp tender. Remove and keep warm. Combine the water, soy sauce, sesame oil, and cornstarch in the skillet. Cook over low heat until the sauce thickens. Return the potatoes and vegetables to the cornstarch mixture in the skillet. Cook and stir over medium heat until mixture is heated through. Spoon onto a serving platter. Garnish with tomato wedges and onions.

Makes about 6 servings.

sweet potato waldorf salad

Sweet potatoes, crunchy apples, crispy celery, grapes, and walnuts make this an easy and colorful salad for perking up fall and winter meals. It's an excellent side dish to serve with poultry, lamb, or pork.

4 medium sweet potatoes
3 large unpeeled red apples, cored and diced
⅔ cup halved red or green seedless grapes
⅔ cup diced celery
⅔ cup chopped walnuts
½ cup orange juice
½ cup plain low fat yogurt
1 tablespoon finely shredded orange peel
1 teaspoon salt
3 cups shredded lettuce

In a large saucepan, cook sweet potatoes, covered, in lightly salted boiling water for 20 to 30 minutes or until tender. Do not overcook. Drain. Cool slightly and peel. Cut sweet potatoes into ½-inch cubes. In a large bowl, combine sweet potatoes, apples, grapes, celery, walnuts, and orange juice. Toss lightly to mix. Cover and chill thoroughly. For dressing, in a small bowl stir together yogurt, orange peel, and salt. Add to salad mixture. Toss lightly to coat. To serve, spoon into lettuce-lined bowl or platter.

Makes about 8 servings.

warm potato and cabbage salad

Shredded cabbage and raisins combined with a sweet-sour dressing give a different taste to hot potato salad. A perfect addition to your barbecue, this dish goes well with either grilled steak or bratwurst (pork sausage of German origin, resembling a pale beige-colored Polish sausage or frank) and your favorite beverage.

1 pound tiny unpeeled new potatoes, halved, or 3 medium red potatoes, peeled and cut into 1-inch cubes
2 tablespoons salad oil
½ cup diced onions
4½ teaspoons flour
4 teaspoons sugar
1 teaspoon salt
½ cup red wine vinegar
½ cup water
¼ teaspoon hot pepper sauce
4 cups shredded cabbage
½ cup raisins
1 tablespoon snipped chives, for garnish

In a large saucepan, cook potatoes, covered, in lightly salted boiling water for 10 to 15 minutes or until tender. Drain. For dressing, in a large nonstick skillet heat oil over medium heat. Add onions and cook for 4 minutes or until tender. Stir in flour, sugar, and salt. Once blended, add wine vinegar, water, and hot pepper sauce. Continue to cook over medium heat, stirring constantly until mixture thickens and comes to a boil. Add potatoes, cabbage, and raisins to dressing mixture. Stir gently to coat salad. Cook over low heat for 5 minutes or until thoroughly heated. Spoon into serving bowl and garnish with chives. Serve immediately.

Makes about 6 servings.

Bleu cheese and almond potato salad

If you enjoy the subtly sharp taste of Bleu cheese, you'll appreciate the distinctive flavor it lends to potato salad. Serve fresh crunchy French or Italian bread with this salad. For dessert, pass a tray of assorted fresh seasonal fruit and enjoy it with a glass of your favorite Port wine.

6 medium unpeeled red potatoes, about 2 pounds
½ cup slivered almonds
½ cup thinly sliced celery
1 4-ounce package crumbled Bleu cheese
¼ cup sliced green onions
2 tablespoons snipped parsley
1 8-ounce carton light dairy sour cream
¼ cup white wine vinegar
1 teaspoon salt
⅛ teaspoon pepper
Lettuce leaves
1 tablespoon dried tomato sprinkles, for garnish
Crumbled Bleu cheese, for garnish

In a large saucepan, cook potatoes in water to cover, about 20 to 25 minutes or just until tender. Drain. Cool slightly. While still warm, peel and cut potatoes into ½-inch cubes. Place almonds in a shallow baking pan. Bake in a 350° oven for 5 to 10 minutes or until they start to brown, stirring once or twice. In a large bowl, combine potatoes, celery, cheese, almonds, onions and parsley. For dressing, in a small bowl combine sour cream, vinegar, salt, and pepper. Pour over potato mixture. Toss lightly. Cover and chill several hours or overnight to allow flavors to blend. Serve in a lettuce-lined bowl topped with dried tomato sprinkles and additional crumbled Bleu cheese.

Makes about 6 to 8 servings.

german potato salad

You'll find many versions of German potato salad across the country. This easy, tangy dish is our family favorite. It's absolutely wonderful in that it tastes great freshly made, and even better if made a day or two ahead with the flavors allowed to develop. Simply reheat it in the oven and serve it with thick, moist slices of baked ham, smoked sausage, or grilled bratwurst.

6 medium unpeeled potatoes, about 2 pounds
1 cup chopped onions
½ pound lean bacon
½ cup cider vinegar
½ cup water
1 egg
1 teaspoon sugar
½ teaspoon salt
¼ teaspoon pepper
1 tablespoon snipped parsley, for garnish

In a covered saucepan, cook potatoes in boiling salted water for about 20 to 25 minutes or just until tender. Drain. Cool slightly. Peel and cut into ¾-inch cubes. Add onions to potatoes and set aside while preparing dressing. Cut bacon into ½-inch pieces. In a large skillet, cook bacon over medium heat until crisp. Remove the bacon with a slotted spoon to paper towels. Let drain. Pour off all but 3 tablespoons of bacon drippings. In a small bowl, whisk together vinegar, water, egg, sugar, salt and pepper. Add vinegar mixture to bacon drippings. Cook and stir over medium heat until bubbly and slightly thickened. Stir in potatoes, onions, and all but 2 tablespoons bacon. Cook for 2 to 3 minutes more or until heated through. Transfer to a serving bowl. Sprinkle top with parsley and reserved bacon.

Makes about 6 servings.

ham 'n cheese potato salad

Cottage cheese is the magic ingredient that makes this potato salad special. Its mild flavor and creamy texture combines happily with the potatoes, ham, and Cheddar cheese. At the same time, it unobtrusively brings out the flavor of the fresh vegetables and herbs. This is an excellent main-dish salad for a light luncheon or informal dinner. Ingredients can be prepared beforehand, chilled and put in a salad bowl just before serving.

2 pounds unpeeled new potatoes
2 cups cubed natural Cheddar cheese
   (8-ounces)
3 cups diced cooked ham (l pound)
1 cup sliced celery
2 hard cooked eggs, chopped
$\frac{1}{4}$ cup sliced green onions
$\frac{1}{4}$ cup chopped green peppers
2 teaspoons snipped fresh dillweed
   OR $\frac{3}{4}$ teaspoon dillweed
1 teaspoon salt
$\frac{1}{8}$ teaspoon pepper
$1\frac{1}{2}$ cups cream-style,
   low fat cottage cheese
$\frac{1}{2}$ cup plain non-fat yogurt
1 tablespoon horseradish sauce
1 medium-size green pepper,
   sliced into rings, for garnish
$\frac{1}{8}$ teaspoon paprika, for garnish

In a covered saucepan, cook potatoes in lightly salted boiling water for 20 to 25 minutes or until tender. Drain. Cool slightly. Peel and cut into $\frac{1}{2}$-inch cubes to make 4 cups. In a large bowl, combine potatoes, Cheddar cheese, ham, celery, eggs, onion, pepper, dill, salt, and pepper. For dressing, in a small bowl stir together cottage cheese, yogurt, and horseradish sauce. Add dressing to salad mixture and toss gently to mix. Cover and chill several hours. Transfer to serving bowl. Garnish with pepper rings and a sprinkle of paprika.

Makes about 8 servings.

"Be eating
one potato,
peeling
a second,
have a third
in your fist,
and your eye
on a fourth."
– Old Irish Saying

spanish potato salad

The celery, red onions, and oranges lend a pleasing visual and flavor excitement to this salad. It's perfect for a cookout and goes beautifully with steak, burgers or grilled chicken.

6 cups cooked and sliced red potatoes,
   about 2 pounds
½ cup celery cut into ¼-inch slices
4 oranges, peeled and sectioned
2 medium red onions, thinly sliced,
   about 2 cups
⅓ cup mayonnaise
⅓ cup sour cream
½ cup orange juice
¼ teaspoon salt
¼ teaspoon hot pepper sauce
Lettuce leaves
1 tablespoon snipped fresh chives
   OR 1 teaspoon dried chives*

In a large bowl, combine potatoes, celery, oranges, and onions. Toss to mix. Cover and chill. For dressing, in a small bowl combine mayonnaise, sour cream, orange juice, salt and hot pepper sauce. Blend until smooth. When ready to serve, pour the dressing over potato mixture. Toss lightly, making sure potatoes, onions and oranges are well coated. Season to taste with additional salt and hot pepper sauce, if desired. To serve, line a platter with lettuce leaves. Arrange salad on lettuce and sprinkle with chives. Serve immediately.

Makes about 8 servings.

new potato-green bean tomato salad

Very small new potatoes are wonderful when complemented with a special blend of mayonnaise, olive oil, and dillweed dressing. Serve with a platter of assorted cold cuts and sliced cheeses along with French bread and herb butter for a satisfying meal on a hot summer day.

1 pound whole small new potatoes,
   unpeeled, halved or quartered
   OR 3 medium red potatoes, cubed
2 cups fresh green beans, trimmed,
   cut into 1½-inch pieces,
   cooked, drained, and chilled
2 cups thinly sliced celery
½ cup chopped onion
4 plum tomatoes, cut into wedges
¼ cup light mayonnaise
2 tablespoons extra virgin olive oil
2 tablespoons snipped fresh dillweed
   OR 2 teaspoons dried dillweed
1 teaspoon salt
⅛ teaspoon pepper
Iceberg lettuce
1 tablespoon snipped parsley

In a large saucepan, cook potatoes, covered, in boiling water for 15 to 20 minutes or just until tender. Drain. Place in a large bowl. Lightly toss green beans, celery, onions, and tomatoes with potatoes. For dressing, in a small bowl combine mayonnaise, olive oil, dill, salt, and pepper. Mix lightly into potato mixture, making sure all vegetables are coated. Cover and chill for at least 3 hours. To serve, line a salad bowl with lettuce. Fill with chilled salad. Sprinkle with snipped parsley just before serving.

Makes about 6 servings.

*Note
Snipped fresh or dried parsley may be substituted for the chives.

confetti potato salad
for a crowd

Wonderful flavors, textures, and colors—an excellent combination. When you bring this dish to your next neighborhood cookout or family get-together, don't be surprised if you're elected the official potato salad maker for the next event. It's excellent served with cold roasts or fried chicken and a big crock of chilled lemonade with lemon or orange slices floating on top.

3 pounds Yukon Gold or red potatoes
½ cup bottled Italian salad dressing
4 hard cooked eggs
¾ cup thinly sliced celery
⅔ cup sliced green onions
1½ cups mayonnaise or salad dressing
½ cup dairy sour cream
1½ teaspoons stone ground mustard
1 teaspoon salt
½ teaspoon prepared horseradish
½ teaspoon celery seed
⅛ teaspoon pepper
⅔ cup peeled and chopped cucumber
⅔ cup chopped tomatoes
1 tablespoon sliced green onion tops

In a large saucepan, cook potatoes, covered, in lightly salted boiling water for 20 to 25 minutes or until tender. Drain. When cool enough to handle, though still warm, peel and slice. In a large bowl, combine potato slices with Italian salad dressing. Toss gently to avoid breaking the potato slices. Cover and chill for 2 hours. Remove egg yolks from egg whites. Chop egg whites. Add the egg whites, celery, and onions to potatoes. Press egg yolks through a sieve. Reserve 2 tablespoons sieved egg yolks for garnish. For dressing, in a small bowl combine egg yolks, mayonnaise, sour cream, mustard, salt, horseradish, celery seeds, and pepper. Pour dressing over potato mixture. Toss lightly to evenly coat. Cover and chill for at least 2 hours to allow flavors to blend. Before serving, stir cucumbers and tomatoes into potato salad. Garnish with reserved egg yolks and sliced green onion tops.

Makes about 10 servings.

old-fashioned potato salad with variations

Bite-size cubes of soft, crumbly russet potatoes tossed together with crisp celery in a creamy dressing makes a moist and sensational potato salad, whether it's served immediately—the way we like it best—or chilled to enjoy later. Either way, it's a versatile dish because you can add a variety of ingredients to change its texture and flavor, yet still be sure of a delicious taste experience.

2 pounds russet or Yukon Gold potatoes, cooked, peeled and cubed
2 hard cooked eggs, sliced
1 cup thinly sliced celery
½ cup diced white onion
1 cup mayonnaise or salad dressing
2 tablespoons cider vinegar
1 teaspoon salt
1 teaspoon sugar
⅛ teaspoon pepper
⅛ teaspoon dry mustard

In a large bowl, combine potatoes, eggs, celery and onions. In a small bowl, whisk together mayonnaise, vinegar, salt, sugar, pepper, and dry mustard. Pour over potato mixture. Gently toss to evenly coat potatoes. Serve immediately or cover and chill potato salad for 2 to 24 hours.

Makes about 8 servings.

Variations

Carrots Add I cup shredded raw carrots.

Cucumbers Add 1 cup peeled and chopped cucumber.

Radishes Add I cup crisp sliced radishes, just before serving.

Pickled Beets Add 1 cup diced pickled beets, just before serving.

Cheese Add 1 cup cubed sharp Cheddar cheese.

Ham, Chicken or Turkey Add 1 cup diced ham, chicken, or turkey.

Sausage Add 1 cup chopped bologna, salami, or Kielbasa.

Bacon Add 8 strips bacon, cooked crisp and crumbled.

Shrimp Add one 4½-ounce can shrimp.

Pickles Add ¼ cup chopped dillweed or sweet pickle.

Red or Green Peppers Add ¼ cup each of chopped peppers for flavor and color.

Olives Add 2 tablespoons chopped or sliced Kalamata, green, stuffed, or ripe olives.

potato-beef moussaka

This Greek-inspired recipe makes a tasty meal, especially when served with a leafy green salad.

Nonstick spray coating
Fine dry bread crumbs
5 medium potatoes
¼ cup butter or margarine, divided
1 large onion, halved and sliced
1½ pounds ground beef
1 clove garlic, minced
3 tablespoons chopped parsley
¼ teaspoon crushed dried thyme
1 teaspoon salt
½ teaspoon pepper
2 tablespoons all-purpose flour, divided
⅓ cup dry white wine
4 eggs
1 cup half-and-half, divided

Preheat oven to 375°. Spray a 2½-quart baking dish with nonstick spray coating and dust with fine, dry bread crumbs. Peel potatoes and cut into ¼-inch slices. Place in cold water. In a large skillet, melt 2 tablespoons butter. Add the onion and sauté until tender. Add ground beef and cook, stirring until browned. Stir in garlic, parsley, thyme, salt, and pepper. Blend in 1 tablespoon of the flour. Add wine and simmer for 5 minutes. Set aside to cool. Separate 2 eggs. In a small bowl, combine 2 egg yolks with the 2 tablespoons of half-and-half. Stir into the meat mixture. Beat 2 egg whites until stiff. Fold into the meat mixture. Drain potatoes thoroughly. In prepared casserole, arrange potatoes and mixture in alternate layers beginning and ending with potatoes. Dot with remaining 2 tablespoons of butter. Bake in preheated oven I hour. Combine remaining eggs, half-and-half and flour. Pour over the top of the casserole. Bake for an additional 15 minutes or until potatoes are tender.

Makes about 6 servings.

main dishes

As wonderful as potatoes are, they become even better when you consider their role in mouthwatering main dishes.

Today, potatoes are grown in all 50 states of the USA and in about 125 countries.

onion steak-potato bake

Serve this tempting, homestyle main dish with a side of butter-glazed tender peas and baby carrots and a tossed green salad.

Nonstick spray coating
3 tablespoons olive oil, divided
3 large onions, thinly sliced
2 cloves garlic, minced
1½ pounds round steak,
    about ½-inch thick
3 tablespoons all-purpose flour
1 cup hot water
2 teaspoons instant beef bouillon granules
6 large potatoes, sliced ¼-inch thick
Salt and pepper to taste
8 tablespoons snipped fresh parsley,
    divided

Preheat oven to 375°. Spray a 3-quart deep baking dish with nonstick spray coating. Set aside. In a large skillet heat 1 tablespoon of olive oil over medium-high heat. Add the onions and garlic. Sauté until golden and tender. Do not brown. Meanwhile, cut steak in 8 pieces. Trim fat. Using a meat mallet, pound the flour into meat, reducing meat to ¼-inch thick. Remove onions from skillet and set aside. Add the remaining oil to the skillet. Brown the meat on both sides in hot oil. Remove and set aside with the onions. Add water and bouillon granules to skillet. Bring to a boil and stir just to loosen pan drippings. Layer half the potatoes in prepared baking dish. Season with salt and pepper. Top with onions and 6 tablespoons parsley. Add the meat. Season with salt and pepper. Top with remaining potatoes. Season with salt and pepper. Add water mixture from the skillet. Cover and bake for 45 minutes. Remove cover and bake for 15 to 20 minutes longer or until meat and potatoes are tender (if dish looks dry at the end of baking, add a small amount of water). Sprinkle with remaining parsley.

Makes about 6 servings.

Note
For convenience, have your butcher tenderize the round steak.

potato gnocchi
with tomato beef sauce

These little potato dumplings are traditional Italian fare. Generally, you'll find them dripping in butter, Parmesan cheese, and/or a delicious sauce. Here, I've added herbs and ground beef to make this a tasty one-dish meal. Serve them with a mixed salad and a fruit dessert.

2 medium russet potatoes,
    peeled and quartered
1 tablespoon butter
1 teaspoon salt
1 egg yolk
¼ cup grated Parmesan cheese
1 cup all-purpose flour

In a medium saucepan, cook potatoes in boiling water until tender. Drain and place in a medium mixing bowl. Beat until smooth. Add butter, salt, egg yolk, and Parmesan cheese. Stir well to mix. Mixing by hand, add flour gradually until dough is stiff. Knead gently for 2 to 3 minutes, adding more flour if necessary, until smooth. Divide dough into quarters. Roll each portion on a lightly floured surface to shape into a sausage ¾-inch thick. Cut into 1-inch pieces. Roll each piece into an oval, then over wires of a slender whisk or dinner fork to make grooves in gnocchi. Arrange gnocchi in a single layer on floured baking sheet. Repeat with remaining dough. Bring a large pot of salted water to boil. Lower gnocchi into the water, in batches of about 20. Remove with a slotted spoon when they rise to the surface after 2 to 3 minutes. Keep warm. Toss with tomato meat sauce and serve with a dusting of Parmesan cheese.

Makes about 6 servings.

tomato beef sauce

1 tablespoon olive oil
1 large onion, chopped
1 clove garlic, minced
1 pound of lean ground beef
1½ cups crushed canned tomatoes
2 tablespoons tomato paste
1 cup water
1 tablespoon shredded fresh basil
½ teaspoon crushed dried thyme
1 teaspoon sugar
1 teaspoon salt
½ teaspoon pepper
1 bay leaf
¼ cup Parmesan cheese, for garnish

Heat oil in a large skillet over medium-high heat. Sauté onion and garlic until golden. Do not brown. Add beef, break up and cook until brown. Add tomatoes, tomato paste, water, basil, thyme, sugar, salt, pepper, and bay leaf. Simmer slowly for 1 hour. To serve, spoon hot sauce over gnocchi. Sprinkle with Parmesan cheese.

Makes about 6 servings.

beef roast with potatoes and onions

There's nothing fancy about this combination. It's simply delicious, reliable, old-fashioned meat and potatoes, just like our mothers prepared.

2 ½-3 pounds chuck roast
2 tablespoons olive oil
¾ cup water, divided
6 medium red potatoes, quartered
3 medium onions, halved
1 teaspoon salt
1 teaspoon pepper

Preheat oven to 350°. Trim fat from roast. In a Dutch oven, over medium-high heat, brown roast on all sides in hot oil. Pour ½ cup water over roast. Cover and place in preheated oven. Bake for 45 minutes. Uncover. Arrange potatoes and onions around roast. Sprinkle with salt and pepper. Bake, basting occasionally, adding more water if necessary, for 60 to 70 minutes or until meat and vegetables are fork tender. Serve with pan juices.

Makes about 6 servings.

rosemary chicken and potatoes

Garnish with flat-leaf parsley and serve accompanied by a green salad.

3 tablespoons olive oil
2 ½-3 pounds meaty chicken pieces (breast halves, thighs, and drumsticks), with skin on
1 medium onion, chopped
2 cloves garlic, minced
¼ pound mushrooms, sliced
1 cup dry white wine
2 teaspoons crushed rosemary
1 bay leaf
4 cups scrubbed medium red potatoes, unpeeled and quartered
2 teaspoons salt
½ teaspoon freshly ground pepper
Flat leaf parsley, for garnish (optional)

Preheat oven to 350°. In a large Dutch oven, heat oil over medium heat. Brown chicken on both sides. Remove browned chicken to side dish. Pour off excess fat. Add onion, garlic and mushrooms to Dutch oven. Sauté until tender. Pour off excess fat, if necessary. Return chicken to Dutch oven. Add wine, rosemary, and bay leaf. Cover and simmer for 5 minutes. Add potatoes, salt, and pepper. Cover and bake in preheated oven for 40 minutes. Remove cover and continue baking for another 20 minutes, or until chicken and potatoes are lightly browned and fork tender. Serve warm garnished with parsley, if desired.

Makes about 4 servings.

tarragon chicken and potatoes

Serve hot for one meal, cold for another; it's equally delicious either way.

Nonstick spray coating
3 pounds of meaty chicken pieces, skinned (breast, thighs and drumsticks)
2/3 cup butter or margarine, divided
1/2 cup Dijon-style mustard
1 teaspoon snipped fresh tarragon
1 1/2 cups fresh breadcrumbs
1/3 cup Parmesan cheese
3 tablespoons fresh snipped parsley, divided
1/8 teaspoon red (cayenne) pepper
6 small unpeeled red potatoes, scrubbed and cut in half

Preheat oven to 350°. Spray a 9" x 13" baking pan with nonstick spray coating. Pat chicken dry. Place in prepared baking pan. In a small saucepan, combine 1/2 cup butter, mustard, and tarragon. Stir over low heat until butter melts. On a sheet of waxed paper or plate, combine breadcrumbs, cheese, 3 tablespoons parsley and red pepper. With a fork, stir to blend. Spoon mustard mixture evenly over chicken, turning pieces to coat on all sides. One at a time, dip chicken in crumb mixture, turning and patting with your fingers to coat evenly. Return each piece to the pan before coating another piece. Place potatoes around chicken pieces. Drizzle remaining butter over the potatoes. Bake in preheated oven for 30 minutes. Turn chicken pieces and continue baking, basting chicken and potatoes with pan juices, for 20 to 25 minutes longer or until chicken is crisp and golden brown and potatoes are fork tender. Remove from oven and place hot chicken on serving platter surrounded by potatoes. Sprinkle remaining parsley over potatoes. Serve immediately.

Makes about 6 servings.

country-style ribs, potatoes and sauerkraut

Here is an easy homestyle flavor dinner combination that's hard to beat, especially when served with caraway rye bread and German style mustard.

1 1/2 pounds country-style pork ribs
1 can (1 pound, 12-ounces) sauerkraut, undrained
1 cup shredded carrot
2 teaspoons caraway seed
1/2 cup water
4 medium potatoes, peeled and quartered
8 bacon slices, cooked crisp and crumbled, for garnish (optional)

Place ribs in a shallow roasting pan and broil for 6 minutes on each side. In a large Dutch oven, combine sauerkraut, carrots, caraway seeds and water. Arrange broiled ribs and potatoes over sauerkraut. Cover and simmer over low heat for 1 1/4 hours or until meat and potatoes are tender. Transfer to a large serving platter. Sprinkle with crisp bacon bits for garnish.

Makes about 4 servings.

In 1664, a book came out dedicated to King Charles II, patron of the new Royal Society, on the subject of potatoes.

potato-topped chili pie

The cheesy potato topping complements the full-flavored chili base.

2 tablespoons olive oil
1½ cups chopped onion
1 cup chopped celery
3 garlic cloves, minced
1½ pounds beef, cut in ¾-inch cubes
1 (28-ounce) can whole peeled tomatoes,
   undrained
1 bay leaf
3 tablespoons chili powder
1 tablespoon Worcestershire sauce
1½ teaspoons cumin
1 teaspoon salt, divided
¼ teaspoon hot pepper sauce
3 medium potatoes,
   scrubbed and cut in half
½ cup warm milk
2 tablespoons butter
1 cup shredded sharp Cheddar cheese
Paprika, for garnish (optional)

In a large skillet, heat oil. Add and sauté onions, celery, and garlic until golden but not browned. Remove from skillet and set aside. Place meat in skillet and brown over medium-high heat. Add the onion mixture, tomatoes, bay leaf, chili powder, Worcestershire sauce, cumin, ¾ teaspoon salt, and hot pepper sauce. Stir to thoroughly blend. Lower heat and simmer, uncovered, about I hour or until meat is tender. If chili mixture thickens too much, cover to retain moisture. Meanwhile, in a large saucepan, cook potatoes in boiling water until just tender. Drain and peel. Preheat oven to 400°. In a large mixing bowl, beat potatoes until smooth. Add milk, butter, remaining salt, and 3/4 cup cheese. Beat until smooth. Place chili mixture into a 2-quart casserole. Carefully spoon potatoes over chili, smoothing out to the edges. Sprinkle with remaining cheese. Garnish with a sprinkle of paprika, if desired. Bake in preheated oven for 15 to 20 minutes or until cheese is melted.

Makes about 4 servings.

greek pouch potatoes

Potatoes prepared in a pouch may not be sophisticated eating, but the flavor of this Greek-inspired dish is quite tasty, especially when topped with chopped tomatoes and Feta cheese. Serve with a salad of leafy greens and red onion rings sprinkled with Vinaigrette dressing.

4 sheets (12-15 inches)
   heavy-duty aluminum foil
Nonstick spray coating
4 medium potatoes, sliced ⅛-inch thick
4 boneless, skinless chicken breast halves,
   sliced ¼-inch thick
1 cup chopped scallions,
   green part included
¾ cup pitted, sliced kalamata olives
   or sliced ripe olives
2 cloves garlic, minced
3 tablespoons lemon juice
1 tablespoon olive oil
2 teaspoons salt
2 teaspoons dried oregano leaves
1 teaspoon pepper
½ cup diced tomatoes
¼ cup crumbled Feta cheese

Preheat oven to 450°. Spray foil sheets with nonstick spray coating and set aside. In a large mixing bowl, combine potatoes, chicken, scallions, olives, garlic, lemon juice, olive oil, salt, oregano, and pepper. Toss to coat all ingredients. Divide the mixture equally among foil sheets. To seal each pouch, bring edges together. Fold in right edge ½-inch, then fold again. Fold top and bottom edges the same way, leaving room for heat to circulate inside pouch. Place on baking sheet and bake in center of oven for 45 to 50 minutes.* To open pouches: with scissors, cut a cross in top of each, then pull back points, being careful as steam is released. Top contents of each pouch with 2 tablespoons tomatoes and 1 tablespoon Feta cheese.

Makes 4 servings.

*Note
Pouches may be grilled for 40 to 45 minutes in covered grill.

barbecue beef pouch potatoes

Here is a handy all-in-one meat and potato meal that's simple to prepare and requires little, if any, cleanup. Add your favorite vegetables, barbecue sauce or seasonings for variety.

4 sheets (12-inches square)
    heavy duty aluminum foil
Nonstick spray coating
4 medium potatoes, cut into ½-inch cubes
1 pound lean ground beef
1 small green pepper, coarsely chopped
½ cup diced onion
½ cup thinly sliced carrots
1 cup prepared hickory smoked
    barbecue sauce

Preheat oven to 450°. Spray foil sheets with nonstick spray coating. In a large mixing bowl, combine potatoes, ground beef, green pepper, onions, and carrots. Add barbecue sauce and toss to coat all ingredients. Divide the mixture equally among foil sheets allowing about 1¾ cups for each. To seal each pouch, fold left side of foil over mixture. Fold in right edge ½ inch. Fold again. Fold top and bottom edges the same way, leaving room for heat to circulate inside pouch. Place on baking sheet and bake in center of oven for 35 to 40 minutes.* To open pouches: with scissors, cut a cross in top of each, then pull back points, being careful not to be burned as steam is released.

Makes 4 servings.

*Note
Pouches may be grilled for 20 to 25 minutes in covered grill.

potato stroganoff

Inspired by the classic Beef Stroganoff. Sour cream, onions, mushrooms, and hamburger combine with potatoes in this recipe to make an unusually delicious one-dish meal.

1 tablespoon butter or margarine
1 large onion, diced
1 clove garlic, minced
½ pound mushrooms, sliced
1 pound lean ground beef
3 medium potatoes, peeled and diced
2 tablespoons flour
1 cup beef broth
2 tablespoons tomato paste
2 teaspoons Worcestershire sauce
1 teaspoon salt
¼ teaspoon pepper
1 cup sour cream
½ cup chopped green onions, for garnish

In a large skillet, heat butter over medium-high heat. Stir in onion and garlic. Cook until golden. Do not brown. Add mushrooms and continue cooking until mushrooms begin to release their liquid. Transfer onion, garlic, and mushrooms to a side dish. Add ground beef to skillet and cook over moderately high heat, for 2 to 3 minutes. Add potatoes and continue cooking until meat is browned and potatoes are tender (for 10 to 12 minutes). Stir in onions, garlic, and mushrooms. Lower heat. Sprinkle flour over meat and stir to blend. Add broth, tomato paste, Worcestershire sauce, salt, and pepper. Stir thoroughly to blend. Adjust seasoning to taste. Blend in sour cream. Simmer until heated through. Do not allow mixture to boil. Serve immediately with green onions sprinkle over the top.

Makes about 6 servings.

spanish potatoes

The generous presence of chili powder is what gives this dish its unique personality. The potatoes and ham, both in flavor and texture, serve to mellow the intense flavor of the chili powder. So be sure to test a sample and make any adjustments to suit your taste.

8 ounces sliced lean bacon
2 large green peppers, diced (about 2 cups)
2 ½ pounds potatoes,
    cubed into bite-sized pieces
    (about 6 cups)
3 cups cubed lean ham
1 can (15-ounces) crushed tomatoes
½ cup chopped Spanish olives
    with pimiento
1 teaspoon onion powder
½ teaspoon garlic powder
2-3 tablespoons chili powder (to taste)
2 cups water
1-2 tablespoons chopped capers*

In a large heavy skillet, cook bacon until well done and crisp. Remove from skillet and drain on paper towel. Crumble and reserve. Pour off all but 1 tablespoon drippings. Add peppers to skillet where you cooked the bacon. Cook for 5 minutes or until pepper is crisp tender. Add potatoes, ham, tomatoes, olives, onion, garlic, chili powder, and water. Bring to boiling and cook uncovered, stirring occasionally, for 20-25 minutes or until potatoes are fork tender. Stir in capers. Let stand 5 minutes to allow liquids to absorb. Stir in crumbled bacon and serve. Sprinkle with additional capers, if desired.

Makes about 8 servings.

german onion-potato scramble

For those who enjoy their morning bacon and eggs, here is a Sunday morning breakfast favorite at our house. We've even been known to serve it for a light evening meal. It's especially delicious when accompanied by a bowl of in-season fruit.

9 slices of lean bacon, diced
2 medium potatoes, peeled and finely diced
    (about 2–2 ½ cups)
1 cup chopped onions
4 eggs, lightly beaten
¼ teaspoon salt
⅛ teaspoon freshly ground pepper
2 tablespoons snipped parsley
⅓ cup shredded Cheddar cheese
    for garnish, optional

In a 10-inch heavy skillet, cook bacon over medium heat until browned and crisp. Remove bacon from pan with a slotted spoon and drain on a paper towel. Pour off all but 3 tablespoons of bacon drippings. To the remaining drippings add potatoes and onions. Sauté over medium low heat, stirring occasionally, until potatoes and onions are tender. Add more bacon drippings if necessary. In a small bowl, lightly beat eggs with salt and pepper. Add the parsley and bacon. Pour over potatoes and onions in skillet. Cover and cook over low heat until eggs are set, for about 5 to 6 minutes. Sprinkle with cheese, if desired. To serve, turn out onto a large platter and cut into wedges.

Makes about 4 servings.

"Potatoes, three pounds a penny, Potatoes Augh fait, here's a kind-hearted lass of green Erin Unruffled in mind, and for trifles not caring Who, trundling her barrow, content in her state is Still crying, three pounds for a penny, Potatoes."
– from a collection of London Street Cries circa 1800

*Additional capers may be used for garnish

side dishes

Some of these great dishes are surprisingly easy to prepare, yet are spectacular enough in flavor and presentation to steal the show.

new potatoes 'n baby onions

Pick out well-shaped small potatoes for pretty presentation. Red, white, blue or even a mixture of varieties will be fine for this recipe. Serve with a leafy green salad and your favorite grilled chicken or fish.

2 pounds new potatoes
1 teaspoon salt
3 tablespoon olive oil
2 teaspoons sesame oil
1 tablespoon soy sauce
2 cups frozen baby onions, thawed
¼ cup dry white wine
¼ cup chicken broth
¾ teaspoon crushed dried red pepper (or to taste)
2 tablespoons plain or toasted sesame seeds*
2 tablespoon snipped fresh parsley, for garnish

In a large saucepan over medium-high heat, cook potatoes in boiling salted water to cover, for 8 to 10 minutes. Drain carefully, leaving skins intact. Keep potatoes warm. In a medium-sized skillet, heat olive oil and sesame oil over medium heat. Stir in soy sauce and onions. Cook, stirring gently, until the onions are tender and slightly browned, for 8 to 10 minutes. Add the potatoes, wine, broth, and crushed pepper. Simmer, shaking the pan occasionally, until the sauce thickens and coats the potatoes and onions, for 2 to 3 minutes. Stir in sesame seeds. Serve immediately, garnished with parsley, if desired.

Makes about 6 servings.

*To toast sesame seeds: Preheat oven to 275°. Place sesame seeds in pie plate. Bake until lightly toasted, stirring occasionally, about 10 minutes. Set aside to cool.

minted new potatoes and peas

This tasty dish from out of the past is an attractive accompaniment to a succulent lamb roast. Use only new potatoes, very fresh herbs, and sweet butter.

2 pounds small new red or white potatoes
1½ teaspoons salt, divided
3 cups fresh or frozen tiny peas
¼ cup butter or margarine
½ cup snipped fresh mint (or to taste)

Scrub the potatoes. Peel strips of skin about ½-inch wide around center of each potato. In a medium saucepan cook potatoes and 1 teaspoon salt in boiling water until fork tender. Do not overcook. Drain. Return to saucepan. In a saucepan, cook peas and ½ teaspoon salt in boiling water just until tender. Drain. If using frozen peas, cook according to package directions. Add to potatoes. In a small saucepan, melt the butter. Add the mint and stir. Pour over hot potatoes and peas and toss gently to thoroughly coat.

Makes about 6 servings.

variation
Parslied New Potatoes and Peas

Prepare as above but substitute 6 tablespoons snipped fresh parsley for the mint.

lemon-buttered blue potatoes

Blue potatoes, found at farmer's markets and specialty food markets, can be steamed, boiled, or baked. However, microwaving preserves their color best. This is an attractive dish with a slight nutty flavor.

1¾ pounds small (not tiny) blue potatoes, unpeeled and halved
¼ cup butter or margarine
2 tablespoons chopped fresh parsley
2 tablespoons lemon juice
1 teaspoon grated lemon rind
1 teaspoon salt
¼ teaspoon pepper
¼ teaspoon nutmeg
¼ cup toasted almonds, for garnish (optional)

Place potatoes in a microwave-safe dish. Microwave, partially covered with vented microwave-safe plastic wrap, on high, for 12 to 15 minutes or until potatoes are tender. Place in a large serving bowl. In a small saucepan, combine butter, parsley, lemon juice, lemon rind, salt and pepper, and nutmeg. Cook over medium heat until butter melts. Pour butter over hot potatoes. Toss to thoroughly coat. Sprinkle with toasted almonds if desired.

Makes about 6 servings.

Drop a few celery leaves, a little onion, and a bay leaf in with your boiling potatoes. They will perk up the flavor of whatever dish you are preparing.

When cooking potatoes, add a bouillon cube to the boiling water. Save the liquid and add it as needed with mashing. This enhances the flavor of the potato, eliminating the need for sour cream or butter for a healthier dish.

dressed fingerlings

Fingerlings are the potatoes to have when you want to eat more than one. While they can be sautéed, roasted, or steamed, I believe the best way to enjoy these golden-fleshed delicacies is the simplest way, boiled and tossed with butter and parsley.

1 pound fingerling potatoes
   (about 2-ounces, 2 to 3-inches long), unpeeled
2 tablespoons butter, at room temperature
1 tablespoon snipped fresh parsley
¼ teaspoon salt
⅛ teaspoon pepper

In a medium saucepan, cook the potatoes in 1 inch of boiling water for about 10 minutes or until just tender when pierced with a fork. Meanwhile, in a small bowl mash together butter, parsley, salt, and pepper. When the potatoes are cooked, drain and place in a serving bowl. Pour the butter mixture over potatoes and toss to coat. If necessary, adjust seasoning to taste. Serve hot.

Makes about 4 servings.

Variation

If desired, replace the parsley in this recipe with your favorite fresh snipped herb, such as chives, mint, or basil.

'tato balls

Nonstick spray coating
1 egg, separated
1 tablespoon instant onion soup mix
3 teaspoons prepared yellow mustard
2 teaspoons dried parsley flakes
1½ cups seasoned very stiff
   mashed potatoes
½ cup shredded Sharp Cheddar cheese
⅔ cup corn flake crumbs
2 tablespoons butter or margarine, melted

Preheat oven to 450°. Spray a large baking pan (a jelly roll pan works fine) with nonstick spray coating. In a small mixing bowl, combine egg yolk, instant onion soup mix, mustard, and parsley. Mix well. Add mashed potatoes and cheese. Stir until thoroughly combined. In a small dish, beat egg white slightly and set aside. Shape potato mixture into balls by level (measuring) tablespoon portions. Dip balls in egg white. Coat evenly with cornflake crumbs. Place on prepared pan, being careful not to crowd. Drizzle with butter. Bake in preheated oven for about 10 minutes or until balls are lightly browned.

Makes about 6 servings, 4 balls per serving.

Variations

Any one of the following may be added to the egg yolk/parsley mixture with the mashed potatoes.

⅓ cup whole kernel corn
⅓ cup crumbled cooked bacon
⅓ cup shredded Pepper Jack cheese
   (omit Cheddar cheese)
¼ cup minced green onions
   (omit parsley flakes and soup mix)
¼ cup grated Parmesan cheese.

baked sweet potatoes and apples

Sure to be a favorite. Try it with pork roast or chops, coleslaw, and a thick slice of Potato Pumpernickel bread.

4 medium sweet potatoes
½ cup brown sugar, firmly packed
¼ cup orange juice
2 teaspoons grated orange rind
1 teaspoon salt
½ teaspoon mace
2 large tart cooking apples, peeled, cored and cut in ½-inch rings
½ cup whole pecans
2 tablespoons butter or margarine

Preheat oven to 350°. Generously butter a 2-quart casserole dish and set aside.

Wash and cook sweet potatoes in boiling water to cover until just tender. Drain. Cool slightly. Peel and cut into crosswise slices ½-inch thick. In a small bowl, combine brown sugar, orange juice, orange rind, salt, and mace. Stir until well blended. In prepared casserole dish, layer one-half of each ingredient at a time: sweet potatoes, apples, pecans, then brown sugar mixture. Repeat, using remaining half of each ingredient. Dot with butter. Cover and bake in preheated oven for 40 to 45 minutes or until apples are tender. Serve warm.

Makes about 6 servings.

german style potatoes and mushrooms

This dish is subtly seasoned, letting the mingled tastes of potatoes and mushrooms dominate. Makes a perfect partner to roast chicken, turkey, veal, pork or fish.

6 medium potatoes, peeled
1 pound fresh mushrooms
4 slices bacon
¾ cup chopped onion
¾ cup sour cream, at room temperature
¾ teaspoon salt
⅛ teaspoon pepper
¼ cup snipped parsley
Paprika, for garnish

Cook potatoes in boiling salted water until just tender. Meanwhile, rinse, pat dry, and slice fresh mushrooms (about 5½ cups). Set aside. Drain, cool, and cut potatoes into 1-inch cubes. Set aside. In a large skillet, cook bacon until crisp. Crumble and set aside. To ¼ cup of bacon drippings left in skillet, add onion and reserved mushrooms. Sauté for 3 minutes or until mushrooms begin to release their liquid. Stir in sour cream, salt, and pepper. Add parsley, reserved potatoes, and bacon. Cook over low heat, stirring gently, until just heated through. Serve warm with a sprinkle of paprika.

Makes about 6 servings.

When trying to save time, slice potatoes and keep them in a bowl of water until you are ready to cook. To prevent them from turning brown, add 2 tablespoons lemon juice for each quart of water. Rinse potatoes and pat dry before cooking.

Combine diced cooked potatoes with crisp-tender broccoli florets. Heat Italian salad dressing and toss with the hot vegetables for a zesty side dish.

caraway potato dumplings

These dumplings are delicious with any roast or stew. They are especially good with sauerkraut and pork dishes.

6 medium white potatoes,
    peeled and cubed
2 eggs, slightly beaten
¾ cup all-purpose flour
½ cup Cream of Wheat™, uncooked
3 tablespoons minced onions
3 teaspoons caraway seeds,
    slightly crushed
1½ teaspoons salt
¼ teaspoon pepper
½ cup toasted breadcrumbs
3 tablespoons snipped fresh chives
    (optional)

In a large saucepan, cook potatoes in boiling water for 20 to 25 minutes or until tender. Drain. Cool slightly. Rice potatoes into a large bowl. Cool to room temperature. Meanwhile, fill a deep saucepan or Dutch oven with 2 quarts of salted water. Heat to boiling while preparing dumplings. Stir eggs, flour, Cream of Wheat, onions, caraway seeds, salt, and pepper into cooled potatoes. Knead dough gently with hands to form soft dough. Rinse hands with cold water. Shape dough into egg-sized balls. Place balls on plate or waxed paper until all are formed. Drop potato balls, one at a time into boiling water. If they do not fit comfortably, cook in two batches. Boil gently for 15 to 20 minutes. Remove dumplings with a slotted spoon to a buttered ovenproof dish. Keep warm in a slow oven (250°) until all are done. To serve, arrange dumplings on a large serving platter, dust with toasted breadcrumbs and a sprinkling of snipped chives if desired.

Makes about 16 dumplings.

Variations

- Add 2 to 3 tablespoons grated sharp Cheddar cheese.

- Omit the caraway seeds and add 6 tablespoons of snipped fresh parsley.

- Leftover dumplings are delicious cut into ½-inch slices and fried in butter or bacon fat.

hungarian paprika potatoes

The paprika lends color, rich flavor and texture to potatoes.

1 large onion, chopped
3 tablespoons butter
6 medium potatoes, peeled and cubed
1 tablespoon sweet Hungarian paprika
1 large green pepper, chopped
1 teaspoon salt
¼ teaspoon pepper
1 cup water, more if necessary

In a heavy saucepan, sauté onion in butter until transparent. Add potatoes, paprika, green pepper, salt, pepper, and 1 cup of water. Continue cooking over low heat until the potatoes are tender, adding a little more water if necessary. Don't stir, but shake the pan occasionally, as stirring can break up the potatoes. Serve warm.

Makes about 6 servings.

hot potato-broccoli vinaigrette

The contrast of cubed potatoes and crisp, tender broccoli is the attraction of this dish. It goes well with roast pork or pork of any kind.

4 medium potatoes,
    peeled and cut into 1-inch cubes
1-1½ pounds broccoli,
    trimmed and broken into small branches
½ cup vegetable oil
¼ cup cider vinegar
1 clove garlic, finely minced
1½ teaspoon salt
1 teaspoon dried basil
⅛ teaspoon hot pepper sauce
2 green onions, sliced
Cherry tomatoes

In saucepan over medium heat, cook potatoes, covered in 1 inch of boiling water until just tender, for 10 to 15 minutes. Drain thoroughly and keep hot. In another saucepan over medium heat cook broccoli, covered, in 1 inch of water until crisp tender, for about 10 minutes. Drain thoroughly and keep hot. In small saucepan, combine oil, vinegar, garlic, salt, basil, pepper sauce, and onions. Bring just to boiling over medium heat, stirring. Arrange hot potatoes and broccoli in serving dish. Pour hot vinegar mixture over and toss gently. Garnish with cherry tomatoes.

Makes about 6 servings.

Brown a little butter and flavor it with cider vinegar. Stir in some snipped parsley and toss with cubes of hot cooked potatoes.

potatoes with sweet red peppers

Pretty as a picture, and tasty enough for a special dinner.

Nonstick spray coating
3 medium potatoes, peeled and cut into ¼-inch slices
2 medium onions, cut into ½-inch slices
2 medium-size sweet red peppers, cut into ½-inch rings
3-ounces thinly sliced smoked ham, shredded
1 clove garlic, minced
1 teaspoon dried leaf rosemary
½ teaspoon salt
¼ teaspoon pepper
¼ cup olive oil
¼ cup snipped parsley

Preheat oven to 375°. Spray a 13" x 9" x 2" baking dish with nonstick spray coating. Set aside. In a large mixing bowl, combine potatoes, onions, red peppers, and ham. Sprinkle with garlic, rosemary, salt and pepper. Pour olive oil over the mixture and toss to coat well. Place mixture in baking dish. Cover with foil and bake for 45 to 50 minutes or until vegetables are tender. Uncover and sprinkle with snipped parsley before serving.

Makes about 8 servings.

basil-garlic potato wedges

If you enjoy cooking outdoors, these grilled potato wedges make a tasty pairing for your burgers, steaks, chicken or pork.

3 large baking potatoes, scrubbed and dried
¼ cup olive oil
1 tablespoon minced garlic
3 tablespoons snipped fresh basil
1 teaspoon salt
Fresh coarse ground pepper, to taste
¼ cup grated Parmesan cheese

Preheat barbecue grill. Cut each potato into 8 lengthwise wedges. In a large bowl, combine olive oil, garlic, basil, salt, and pepper. Add potatoes and toss to coat evenly. Arrange potato wedges over direct heat on hot grill. Cook until fork tender, for about 3 to 4 minutes on each side or until potatoes are golden brown. Carefully remove and place on serving dish. Gently toss with cheese. Serve hot.

Makes about 6 servings.

Variation

2 tablespoons of snipped fresh rosemary may be substituted for the basil in this recipe.

potato pancakes

For breakfast, lunch, or dinner, these crispy pancakes make a tasty meal, especially when served with a dollop of sour cream, chopped ripe olives, a generous slice of ham, and a serving of applesauce on the side.

**4 medium potatoes, peeled
(about 1⅓ pounds)
1 medium onion
½ teaspoon salt
¼ cup chopped and pitted ripe olives
¼ cup finely diced green pepper
¼ cup finely diced sweet red pepper
2 eggs, slightly beaten
2 tablespoon all-purpose flour
⅛ teaspoon pepper
¼ cup cooking oil
½ cup dairy sour cream,
for garnish (optional)
Chopped and pitted black olives,
for garnish (optional)
Line a baking sheet with paper towels
and set aside.**

Finely shred potatoes into a bowl of cold water. Drain. Finely shred onion. Add to potatoes along with salt. Place the potato mixture in a colander set over a large bowl. Let mixture stand for 15 minutes, stirring occasionally. Press the potato mixture firmly to remove as much liquid as possible. Discard the liquid. Transfer the potato mixture to a large mixing bowl. Stir in olives and peppers. In a small mixing bowl, combine the eggs, flour, and pepper. Add to the potato mixture. Stir to thoroughly blend. Heat oil in a heavy skillet over medium heat until hot (add additional oil as needed). For each pancake, drop about ¼ cup potato mixture onto the skillet. Spread mixture into a circle about 4 inches in diameter. Cook over medium heat for 4 to 5 minutes or until pancakes are crisp and golden brown (reduce heat if pancakes are browning too fast). Drain pancakes briefly on prepared baking sheet. Serve immediately or keep warm in a closely covered ovenproof dish in a 300° oven. If desired, garnish with sour cream and black olives.

Makes about 9 pancakes.

potato zucchini curry

This is an attractive dish that goes well with barbecued beef or pork ribs. The spice blend of turmeric, cumin and coriander gives this dish its curry flavor.

3 tablespoons butter or margarine
1 teaspoon dry mustard
1 teaspoon ground turmeric
¾ teaspoon ground cumin
¾ teaspoon coriander
½ teaspoon salt
¼ teaspoon ground red pepper
3 large red potatoes,
   peeled and cubed (3 cups)
1 large zucchini, sliced (2 cups)
2 large plum tomatoes,
   seeded and chopped

In a large skillet, melt butter or margarine over moderate heat. When butter sizzles, stir in mustard, turmeric, cumin, coriander, salt and red pepper. Reduce heat to low. Cook and stir for 5 minutes. Stir in potatoes, making sure all are well coated. Cover and cook for 15 to 20 minutes or until tender, stirring occasionally. Stir in zucchini. Cover and cook for 4 to 5 minutes or until vegetables are tender. Stir in tomatoes. Continue cooking until heated through.

Makes about 8 servings.

mashed and baked

Eeny, meeny, miney, mo... it's difficult to pick a favorite. Will it be a cloud of rich, creamy mashed potatoes, or heaps of fluffy white or yellow potato, bursting from a snug brown jacket? Either way, you've picked a winner.

- To keep mashed potatoes from developing a "gummy" texture, don't over-beat them.

- Drop leftover mashed potatoes into serving-size muffin cups and freeze them. Once they're frozen, place them in resealable plastic bags. During the week, pull out as many servings as needed and heat them in the microwave.

- Boil peeled and quartered potatoes in milk until tender for extra satisfying mashed potatoes. Drain and set the milk aside. Season the potatoes to taste with salt, pepper, and butter, then beat in the hot reserved milk until moist and smooth.

- The floury potatoes, such as russets, are best for mashing. To mash, use a potato masher, ricer, or electric mixer. Don't use a food processor or they will be gummy.

- To help fluff your mashed potatoes, add a pinch or two of baking powder.

- **All-Purpose Thickener:** To thicken soup or stew, mix leftover mashed potatoes into the liquid, a small amount at a time, until desired consistency is reached.

Do the International Mash

- Mash potatoes with mint leaves, as in India.

- For Middle Eastern flavor, mash potatoes with nuts and cinnamon.

- Mashing potatoes with kale makes the Irish/Scottish delicacy *colcannon*.

- Add olive oil, vinegar, and garlic to cold mashed potatoes to make the Greek dip or sauce called *skordalia*.

- Ecuadorians stuff seasoned mashed potatoes with Muenster cheese, pat them into cakes, then fry them to a golden brown in a favorite mountain dish, *llapingachos*.

basic mashed potatoes

This is the ultimate in soul-satisfying comfort food. If you want a simple mashed potato recipe, start here. Creamy mashed potatoes welcome any number of variations. For best results, use firm, mature—not new—potatoes for mashing.

6 medium potatoes, peeled and quartered
4 tablespoons butter
½-⅔ cup hot milk or half-and-half
Salt and freshly ground white pepper,
**   to taste**

In a large saucepan, cover potatoes with cold water. Add a generous pinch of salt. Bring to boiling. Partially cover and reduce heat to medium; cook until potatoes are fork tender. Drain potatoes and return to heat for a few seconds to dry. Put potatoes through a ricer or mash them with a hand masher until perfectly smooth. Beat the butter into the potatoes with a wooden spoon. Meanwhile, heat the milk in the pan and add gradually to the potatoes until they are the desired consistency. You may not need all the milk, depending on how thirsty the potatoes are. Season with salt and pepper. Serve warm.

Makes about 6 servings.

Variations

- **Broccoli and Mashed Potatoes**
  Add small broccoli florets to cooking water during the last 10 minutes of boiling. Mash with the potatoes. Serve with a sprinkling of shredded Cheddar cheese.

- **Dijon-Herb Mashed Potatoes**
  Stir 1 to 2 tablespoons coarse grain or regular Dijon-style mustard and 1 to 2 tablespoons snipped fresh herbs, such as thyme or basil, into mashed potatoes.

- **Balsamic-Mashed Potatoes**
  Drizzle a little balsamic vinegar into your mashed potatoes for a little zip. This makes a perfect match for a big, juicy hamburger or sizzling steak.

garlic-parmesan
mashed potatoes

**Rich and creamy, mashed potatoes
don't get much better than this!**

3 tablespoons butter, divided
1 clove garlic, minced
4 cups mashed potatoes
2 cups half-and-half
1 egg yolk
½ cup freshly grated Parmesan cheese
1 teaspoon salt
⅛ teaspoon freshly ground black pepper
Paprika, for garnish

In a medium saucepan, melt butter.
Add garlic and sauté until golden, but not
browned. Add mashed potatoes and half-
and-half. Stir to blend. Cook and stir for
6 minutes over medium-high heat to allow
potatoes to absorb the half-and-half. Lower
heat. Stir in egg yolk. Continue cooking for
another 3 minutes. Stir in Parmesan cheese,
salt and pepper and remaining butter.
Let stand for 2 to 3 minutes. Serve warm
with a sprinkle of paprika.

Makes about 6 servings.

mashed potatoes
with horseradish cream

Serve with your favorite pot roast.

4 large russet potatoes
1¼ teaspoon salt, divided
3 tablespoons butter, melted, divided
Freshly ground pepper
½ cup sour cream
1 tablespoon prepared horseradish
1 teaspoon fresh snipped parsley
Paprika, for garnish (optional)

In a large saucepan, cook potatoes in boiling
water with ¼ teaspoon salt, until fork
tender. Drain. Sprinkle with remaining salt.
Shake the saucepan over low heat until
potatoes are dry and mealy. Mash, adding 2
tablespoons butter and pepper. Whisk in
sour cream, horseradish and parsley until
blended. Serve topped with remaining butter
and a dash of paprika, if desired.

Makes about 4 servings.

Some cooks claim potatoes mashed with buttermilk instead of milk are the best they've ever tasted.

garlic 'n sweet pepper mashed potatoes

Think of yellow, orange, red, and green sweet peppers to add eye appeal, crisp, tender texture, and tempting flavor the next time you want to add variety to your mashed potatoes. Serve with roast chicken or baked chicken breasts.

4 large russet or Yukon Gold potatoes,
    peeled and quartered
2 large garlic cloves, unpeeled
1¼ teaspoons salt, divided
1 tablespoon olive oil
⅓ cup diced yellow pepper
⅓ cup diced orange pepper
⅓ cup diced red pepper
⅓ cup diced green pepper
½ cup warm milk
3 tablespoons butter, divided
⅛ teaspoon freshly ground black pepper
1 teaspoon snipped parsley for garnish,
    (optional)

In a medium saucepan, cook potatoes, garlic and ¼ teaspoon salt in boiling water until tender. Drain well. Return potatoes to the pan. Shake the pan over low heat until potatoes are dry and mealy. While the potatoes are cooking, heat the olive oil in a small skillet over medium heat. Add the yellow, orange, red and green peppers. Sauté, stirring constantly, for 3 to 4 minutes or until crisp tender. Do not brown. Put the potatoes and garlic through a ricer or mash with a hand masher until smooth. Whisk in the warm milk, butter and pepper. Continue to whisk until the potatoes are fluffy. Blend in the peppers, adding more milk if necessary. Transfer to a serving bowl, making a well in the center of the mixture. Place the remaining butter into the well with a sprinkle of parsley, if desired.

Makes about 4 servings.

mashed potatoes with sauerkraut

Here is a somewhat surprising but wonderful combination. Your family and guests will enjoy this with either broiled pork loin chops or with sizzling sausages and a bowl of applesauce on the side.

2 tablespoons butter or margarine
1 medium yellow onion,
    halved and thinly sliced
2 cloves garlic, minced
¼ cup dry white wine
1-1½ cups chicken broth
1 teaspoon crushed caraway seeds
1 pound refrigerated sauerkraut,
    rinsed, drained, and squeezed dry
4 cups seasoned mashed potatoes
Salt and freshly ground white pepper,
    to taste

In a large nonstick skillet, melt the butter over medium heat. Add the sliced onion and cook until softened and lightly browned, stirring occasionally. Add the garlic, wine, ½ cup of the broth, and caraway seeds. Stir to blend and continue cooking for 5 minutes longer. Stir in sauerkraut and enough remaining broth to barely cover the contents. Simmer, covered, for 30 to 40 minutes, stirring occasionally, until sauerkraut is tender, lightly browned, and liquid has been absorbed. Add and blend into the mashed potatoes. Season to taste. Serve warm.

Makes about 6 servings.

mashed potatoes and butternut squash

Butternut squash's naturally sweet flavor goes well with mashed potatoes and roasted meats. Be sure to use a light hand when blending the potatoes and chunks of golden squash. The combination of flavors and colors makes this an attractive dish.

1 small butternut squash,
   halved lengthwise,
   seeds and fiber removed
½ cup water
5 medium russet potatoes,
   peeled and quartered
3 tablespoons butter, softened
½ cup sour cream
2 teaspoons of red wine vinegar
Freshly grated nutmeg
¼-½ cup hot milk, as needed
5 slices bacon, cut into ¼-inch dice
½ small onion, diced
½ small green pepper, diced
Salt and pepper to taste
¼ cup snipped fresh chives for garnish
   (optional)

Preheat oven to 400°. Place the squash, cut side down, in a shallow baking dish large enough to hold the squash in a single layer. Add the water to the pan. Bake, uncovered, for 30 minutes. Remove the dish from the oven, turn the squash over and cool. Meanwhile, in a large saucepan, cover the potatoes with cold water. Add a generous pinch of salt. Bring to boiling. Partially cover and reduce heat to medium; cook until potatoes are fork tender. Drain potatoes and return to the saucepan. Mash the potatoes with a hand masher until smooth and lump-free. Beat in the butter, sour cream, vinegar, and a grating or two of nutmeg. If the mashed potato mixture is stiff, gradually add a small amount of hot milk until desired consistency is reached. In a small heavy skillet, over medium heat, fry the bacon until crisp. Remove the bacon from the skillet with a slotted spoon and drain on paper towels. Add the onion and green pepper to the bacon fat in the skillet and cook, stirring until the vegetables are just translucent. Remove the onions and pepper with a slotted spoon and drain on paper towels. Add the bacon, onion, and green pepper to mashed potatoes. Beat with a wooden spoon until the mixture is fluffy. Peel the skin from the squash, cut the flesh into chunks, and stir into the potatoes. Try to leave the squash in chunks, if possible. Season with salt and pepper to taste. Serve warm with a sprinkle of snipped chives.

Makes about 8 servings.

refrigerator mashed potatoes

This make-ahead recipe for mashed potatoes was inspired by my friend, Ruth. She says it's a perfect way to cut down on the last-minute serving rush for holiday meals and family gatherings.

8 to 10 russet potatoes,
   peeled and quartered
1 (8-ounce) package cream cheese,
   softened
1 cup sour cream
2 tablespoons fresh snipped chives
1½ teaspoons onion salt, to taste
1 teaspoon salt
¼ teaspoon garlic powder, to taste
¼ teaspoon pepper
2 tablespoons butter or margarine
Nonstick spray coating

In a large saucepan, cook potatoes with a generous pinch of salt in boiling water until tender. Drain and mash with a hand masher until smooth. Add cream cheese, sour cream, chives, onion salt, salt, garlic powder, pepper, and butter. Beat with a wooden spoon until light and fluffy. Spray a 9" x 13" baking dish with nonstick spray coating. Place potatoes in prepared baking pan. Cover and refrigerate. Just before you're ready to eat them, preheat oven to 350°. Bake the mashed potatoes, covered, for 45 minutes or until heated through. Remove the cover. Bake for 15 to 20 minutes longer to crisp and brown the top. Do not stir. Serve warm in the pan.

Makes about 12 servings.

jalapeño-ham stuffed potatoes

Tastes and textures mingle in this blend of baked potatoes, jalapeño-studded Monterey Jack cheese, ham, and a light touch of crushed red pepper.

4 large russet potatoes,
   scrubbed and wiped dry
2 tablespoons butter or margarine
¾ cup finely diced ham
1 cup shredded Monterey Jack cheese
   with jalapeño peppers
1½ cups sour cream, divided
½ teaspoon crushed red pepper flakes
½ teaspoon salt
⅛ teaspoon garlic powder
⅛ teaspoon pepper
3 tablespoons snipped fresh chives
   for garnish, if desired

Preheat oven to 425°. Pierce the skin of each potato in several places with fork tines. Place potatoes in a preheated oven, directly on the rack and bake for 45 to 60 minutes, depending on the size of the potatoes. Potatoes are done when a knife inserted in the center tests soft or when squeezed gently with a mitted hand, they "give" slightly. Cut the baked potatoes in half lengthwise. Scoop out the pulp leaving ¼-inch skin. Reserve skins. In a medium mixing bowl, mash potatoes with a fork. Add butter, ham, cheese, sour cream, pepper flakes, salt, garlic powder, and pepper. Beat with a wooden spoon until well blended. Spoon mixture into reserved potato skins. Return to oven and bake at 375° for 20 minutes or until filling is heated through and browned on top. Serve warm with a dollop of remaining sour cream and a sprinkling of chives, if desired.

Makes 4 servings.

twice-baked potatoes with blended cheese

Looking for something just a bit different? Try fluffy baked potatoes with your favorite blended cheese combination, such as the garlic Italian blend called for in this recipe.

6 large baking potatoes, scrubbed and dried
¼ cup butter, melted
I cup finely chopped onion
I cup finely chopped green pepper
1 small clove garlic, minced (optional)
½ cup milk
1 teaspoon salt
⅛ teaspoon pepper
1 cup shredded Garlic Italian Blend cheese, divided

Preheat oven to 425°. Pierce the skin of each potato in several places with fork tines. Place potatoes in a preheated oven directly on the rack and bake for 45 to 60 minutes, depending on the size of the potatoes. Potatoes are done when a knife inserted in the center tests soft or when squeezed with a mitted hand will "give" slightly. Cut the baked potatoes in half length-wise. Scoop out the pulp leaving ¼-inch skin. Reserve skins. In a medium mixing bowl mash potatoes with a fork. In a small saucepan, combine melted butter, onion, green pepper, and minced garlic. Cook until tender. Add milk and cook until slightly heated. Whisk into mashed potatoes. Blend in salt, pepper, and ½ cup of cheese. Spoon mixture into potato shells. Top with remaining cheese. Bake for 10 to 15 minutes or until filling is heated through and lightly browned. Serve warm.

Makes about 6 servings.

reuben spuds

An easy-to-make entrée for lunch or a light supper.

Nonstick spray coating
4 medium potatoes, scrubbed and dried
¾ cup bottled Russian-style dressing
8 thin slices of corned beef
1½ cups sauerkraut, drained
¾ teaspoon crushed caraway seeds, divided
8 slices Swiss cheese

Preheat oven to 425°. Spray a 9" x 13" shallow baking pan with nonstick spray coating. Pierce the skin of each potato in several places with fork tines. Place potatoes in a preheated oven, directly on the rack, and bake for 45 to 60 minutes, depending on the size of the potatoes. To test for doneness, insert a knife in the potato's center to test for softness, or squeeze gently with a mitted hand until you feel it "give" slightly. Cut the baked potatoes in half lengthwise. Place the potato halves split-side up in prepared baking pan. Spread each hot half evenly with dressing. Top potato with corned beef and sauerkraut. Sprinkle with ½ teaspoon caraway seeds. Layer on cheese slices. Return to hot oven. Bake for 5 to 10 minutes longer or until cheese melts and sauerkraut is heated through. Serve immediately with a sprinkling of the remaining caraway seeds.

Makes about 4 servings.

A large baked potato has twice the potassium of a medium banana.

Note
Garlic Italian blend cheese can be found in cheese specialty stores. If it is not available, your favorite shredded cheese can be substituted.

salmon-stuffed potatoes with dilly cream sauce

This surprising mingling of flavors paired with peas makes a family-pleasing meal.

4 large russet potatoes,
   scrubbed and wiped dry
1 can (7¾ ounces) salmon
   OR 1 cup canned salmon
Milk
2 tablespoons butter, softened
1 egg, slightly beaten
3 tablespoons grated Parmesan cheese
¼ teaspoon salt
⅛ teaspoon pepper
3 tablespoon minced green onions
Dilly Cream Sauce*

Preheat oven to 425°. Pierce the skin of each potato in several places with fork tines. Place potatoes in a preheated oven, directly on the rack, and bake for 45 to 60 minutes, depending on the size of the potatoes. Potatoes are done when a knife inserted in the center tests soft or when squeezed gently with a mitted hand, they "give" slightly. Cut the baked potatoes in half lengthwise. Scoop out pulp leaving ¼-inch skin. Reserve skins. In a medium mixing bowl mash potatoes with a fork. Drain and flake salmon, reserving liquid. Add enough milk to salmon liquid to make ¼ cup. Add liquid, butter, egg, cheese, salt, and pepper to mashed potatoes. Beat with a wooden spoon until well blended. Fold in flaked salmon and green onions. Spoon mixture into reserved potato shells. Return potatoes to oven and bake at 375° for 20 minutes or until filling is heated through and lightly browned. Serve with Dilly Cream Sauce.

Makes about 4 servings.

*dilly cream sauce

2 tablespoons butter or margarine
1 package (10 ounces) frozen peas, thawed
1 cup sour cream
2 tablespoons milk
½ teaspoon dried dillweed
¼ teaspoon salt

In a medium skillet melt butter over low heat. Add peas, sour cream, milk, dillweed and salt. Cook for 3 minutes over low heat until mixture begins to bubble. Remove from heat. Serve immediately over salmon stuffed potatoes.

Makes about 3 cups.

baked potatoes

The perfect baked potato has a dry, crusty skin and is fluffy and mealy inside. Best of all, they are simple to prepare.

4 medium potatoes, preferably russets, skins on and scrubbed
Salt and pepper to taste
Butter (optional)
Sour cream (optional)
Toppings

Preheat oven to 425°. Pierce the skin of each potato in several places with fork tines. This will allow steam to escape and prevent the potato from bursting. Place the potatoes in a preheated oven, directly on the rack and bake for 45 to 60 minutes, depending on the size of the potatoes. If other foods are baking in the oven at the same time, at higher or lower temperatures, adjust the potato baking time accordingly. Potatoes are done when a knife inserted in the center will test soft or when squeezed gently with a mitted hand, they "give" slightly. To serve, "blossom" the potato by making an "X" on the top of the potato with fork tines. Gently squeeze the potato from both ends and fluff the pulp. Pass the salt and pepper, plenty of butter or sour cream, if desired, or top with your favorite toppings.

Makes 4 servings.

seasoned butters for baked potatoes

It's easy to vary baked potatoes with classic sour cream and chives. Interesting, too, is a seasoned butter to top the baked potato and melt down into the fluffy, textured interior.

Onion Butter
Cream ½ cup soft butter or margarine with 4 teaspoons grated onion.

Horseradish Butter
Cream ½ cup soft butter or margarine with 4 tablespoons drained prepared horseradish.

Herb Butter
Cream ½ cup butter or margarine with ¼ teaspoon each dried leaf basil, tarragon, and thyme.

Note
- Do not wrap potatoes in foil to bake, as this will give you soggy, "steamed" potatoes.
- For a softer potato skin, rub with olive or vegetable oil before baking.
- For a crustier potato skin, bake longer in a hotter oven.
- To reheat a baked potato, dip it in cold water and bake it in a preheated 350° oven for 20 minutes.
- Use leftover baked potatoes to make great home fries.

assorted hot toppings for baked potatoes

Quantities are appropriate for 4 servings.

spicy sausage Topping

1 tablespoon olive oil
¾ cup finely chopped onion
1 clove garlic, minced
1 pound bulk hot Italian sausage
¼ teaspoon crush oregano leaves

In a medium skillet, heat oil and sauté onion and garlic until tender. Add and blend in sausage and oregano. Cook, stirring occasionally, on medium heat for 10 minutes, or until sausage is well browned. Drain off excess fat. Cut or pierce center of baked potatoes lengthwise. Squeeze ends and push toward center to fluff the potato open. Top each with ¼ of sausage mixture.

Makes about 4 servings.

spinach topping

2 tablespoons butter or margarine
1 10-ounce package frozen chopped
   spinach, thawed and squeezed dry
1 cup sour cream
Dash of ground nutmeg
Salt and pepper to taste

In a small saucepan, heat butter over medium-low heat. Add spinach. Cook, stirring occasionally for 5 minutes. Lower heat and add sour cream and nutmeg. Cook and stir for 2 minutes. Add salt and pepper to taste. Cut or pierce top of baked potato lengthwise. Squeeze ends and push toward center to fluff the potato open. Top with ¼ of spinach topping.

Makes about 4 servings.

other toppings for baked potatoes

- Sour cream sprinkled with your favorite seasoning blends

- Spicy salsa

- Snipped parsley, basil, chives, thyme, or dillweed

- Your favorite variety of shredded cheese (Cheddar, Swiss, Pepper Jack, Monterey Jack or other great melting cheese)

- Sour cream and chopped green onions

- Yogurt and snipped chives

- Crumbled crisply fried bacon

- Chopped olives

- Freshly grated Parmesan cheese

- Creamy salad dressing

shrimp and dillweed topping

1 tablespoon olive oil
½ cup chopped onion
1½ cups cooked, peeled salad shrimp
⅔ cup seafood cocktail sauce
1 tablespoon lemon juice
¾ teaspoon dried dillweed
¾ teaspoon sugar

In a small nonstick skillet, heat oil and sauté onion until tender. Add shrimp, cocktail sauce, lemon juice, dillweed , and sugar. Cook and stir until shrimp mixture is thoroughly heated. Cut or pierce top of baked potatoes lengthwise. Squeeze ends and push toward center to fluff potatoes open. Top each with ¼ of shrimp and dillweed topping.

Makes about 4 servings.

creamy chicken curry topping

1 tablespoon olive oil
⅓ cup diced onion
½ cup diced celery
⅓ cup flour
1 teaspoon curry powder
¾ teaspoon salt
Freshly ground pepper, to taste
1 cup chicken broth
⅓ cup milk
1⅓ cups cooked, diced chicken or turkey

In a medium saucepan, heat olive oil and sauté onion and celery until crisp tender. Stir in flour, curry powder, salt, and pepper. Continue to cook and stir for 1 minute or until well blended. Slowly blend in broth. Add milk. Cook and stir until thickened. Add chicken or turkey and continue to cook until chicken is heated through. Cut or pierce tops of baked potatoes lengthwise. Squeeze ends and push toward center to fluff potatoes open. Top with ¼ of the creamy chicken curry topping.

Makes about 4 servings.

sesame herb roasted potatoes

This is a simple way to prepare potatoes. They are a perfect complement to your sizzling steaks. Serve with a bibb lettuce salad and a basket of dinner rolls.

Nonstick spray coating
¼ cup sesame seeds
3 tablespoons Mexican Seasoning blend
   OR your favorite seasoning blend
1 tablespoon dried parsley
6 medium Yukon Gold potatoes, peeled and wiped dry
1 tablespoon olive oil
Butter (optional)
Sour cream (optional)

Preheat oven to 400°. Spray a 9" square baking pan with nonstick spray coating. In a small bowl, combine sesame seeds, Mexican seasoning blend, and parsley. Rub potatoes lightly with olive oil. Roll potatoes in sesame seed mixture to coat well. Arrange potatoes in prepared baking pan. Bake in preheated oven, shaking pan occasionally to turn potatoes, for 50 to 60 minutes or until potatoes test done when pierced with a fork. Serve warm topped with butter or sour cream, if desired.

Makes about 6 servings.

Variation

Cheesy Roasted Potatoes
Prepare as directed, but substitute grated Parmesan or Romano cheese for the sesame seeds and Mexican Seasoning blend. Serve with a sprinkling of paprika.

roasted and fried

You only need two words to describe roasted and fried potatoes: unpretentious and delicious. Of course, if you want to add irresistible, I won't disagree.

oven roasted potato wedges

Quick and easy, just the thing when you're in a rush to serve dinner.

Nonstick spray coating
2 large russet potatoes
1 tablespoon olive oil
1 tablespoon butter, melted
2 teaspoons lemon and pepper
   seasoning salt
3 tablespoons grated Parmesan cheese
1 tablespoon snipped parsley
1 tablespoon chopped green onions
Paprika, for garnish (optional)

Preheat oven to 400°. Spray a cookie sheet with nonstick spray coating. Scrub potatoes. Cut lengthwise into 6 to 8 wedge slices and place on cookie sheet. In a small bowl, combine oil, butter, lemon and pepper seasoning salt. Blend and brush on wedges. Sprinkle with cheese. Bake in preheated oven for 20 to 25 minutes or until potatoes are lightly brown and tender. Sprinkle wedges with parsley and green onions and a dash of paprika before serving.

Makes about 4 servings.

hasselback potatoes

Hasselback potatoes—an attractive, easy to prepare dish—complements any meat, fish, or poultry main course with just a salad.

Nonstick spray coating
4 medium even waxy potatoes, peeled
2-3 tablespoons melted butter
4 tablespoons chopped fresh chives
Coarse salt and freshly grated pepper
4 tablespoons grated Cheddar cheese
1 tablespoon fine dry bread crumbs
½ teaspoon sweet Hungarian paprika

Preheat oven to 425°. Spray a shallow 9" ovenproof dish with nonstick spray coating. To cut, place a potato in the hollow of a deep wooden spoon large enough to hold the potato firmly so it can be sliced. Using a small, sharp knife, beginning ½ inch from one end, carefully make ⅛-inch thick slices into the potato. Do not cut all the way through. Slices will fan out slightly. Repeat with the remaining potatoes. Place potatoes, cut side up, in prepared baking dish. Generously brush the entire surface of each potato with melted butter. Sprinkle the tops with snipped chives, followed by salt and pepper. Roast the potatoes, uncovered, for 40 to 50 minutes or until potatoes are golden brown and test tender when pierced with a fork. Remove baking dish from oven. Drizzle any of the remaining butter over the potatoes. Sprinkle with combined Cheddar cheese and breadcrumbs. Return dish to oven and continue baking for another 15 minutes or until cheese is golden brown and melted. Remove the dish from the oven. Sprinkle a strip of paprika down the center of each potato. Serve immediately.

Makes about 4 servings.

Note
You can substitute fresh parsley, thyme, or sage for the chives in this recipe or use 2 to 3 teaspoons of your favorite dried herbs.

balsamic-roasted potatoes

Potatoes love the company of spices. The addition of balsamic vinegar adds depth to the flavorful combination.

2 pounds small new red potatoes, washed, patted dry, and quartered OR 6 medium red potatoes, washed, patted dry, and cut into 1-inch pieces
2 tablespoons light olive oil
2 tablespoons minced onion
1 tablespoon minced garlic
1 teaspoon dried thyme
1 teaspoon dried rosemary
⅛ teaspoon freshly grated nutmeg
¼ cup balsamic vinegar
Salt and pepper

Preheat oven to 400°. In a large bowl, combine potatoes with olive oil, onion, garlic, thyme, rosemary, and nutmeg. Toss until well mixed. Spray a 10" x 15" baking sheet with nonstick spray coating. Arrange potatoes in a single layer in baking pan. Place pan in preheated oven on lower rack. Roast potatoes for 35 to 45 minutes or until tender, stirring midway. Sprinkle the vinegar over potatoes and toss well. Season with salt and pepper. Serve immediately.

Makes about 6 servings.

potato fans

Here is a simple but attractive crisp and tasty garnish for the next time you serve a roast.

Nonstick spray coating
2 large oval shaped russet potatoes
2 tablespoons olive oil
Coarse salt
Freshly ground black pepper

Preheat oven to 550°. Spray a cookie sheet with nonstick spray coating. Wash, scrub and pat the potatoes dry. Cut the potatoes into thin, lengthwise slices. Keep the slices in place as you cut. Divide the slices into groups of four. Place on prepared cookie sheet. Fan out each portion to form four semi-circles of overlapping potatoes. The closer they are fanned together, the better they will hold their shape. Gently brush exposed surfaces of potatoes with olive oil. Lightly sprinkle with salt and pepper. Bake in preheated oven for 10 minutes. Remove from oven. Gently brush potato slices with additional olive oil. Return to oven for 8 to 10 minutes or until potatoes are lightly browned and tender. Carefully remove potato fans to serving side dish with a pancake turner or wide spatula.

Makes about 4 servings.

French fries are popular around the world. Americans dip theirs in ketchup. The English and Canadians shake vinegar on their fries. In Holland and Belgium, fries are served in small paper cones with a dollop of mustard mayonnaise. In Spain, pepper adds spice.

oven roasted sweet potatoes with tarragon

A delicious complement to roast pork or grilled chicken.

Nonstick spray coating
2 medium sweet potatoes, washed and scrubbed
1½ tablespoons olive oil
1 tablespoon snipped fresh tarragon
¾ teaspoon salt
⅛ teaspoon pepper
Paprika, for garnish (optional)

Preheat oven to 475°. Spray a 10½" x 15½" baking pan with nonstick spray coating. Slice sweet potatoes into very thin rounds. Place rounds in a single layer in prepared baking pan. Toss with olive oil, tarragon, salt and pepper. Roast in preheated oven on middle rack, stirring occasionally, for 30 to 35 minutes or until potatoes are crisp and lightly brown. Serve warm, with a sprinkle of paprika if desired.

Makes about 4 servings.

swiss potato-onion cake

Here is a good way to use up leftover boiled potatoes. However, you can also start from scratch, just as long as you chill the potatoes before shredding them. I like to serve this for a hearty brunch or supper, along with a rib-eye steak and leafy salad.

Nonstick spray coating
1½ cups chopped sweet Spanish onions
½ cup diced sweet red pepper
2 tablespoons butter or margarine
2 pounds potatoes, cooked, chilled, and shredded (about 4½ cups)
2 cups shredded Swiss cheese
⅓ cup sliced black olives
1 teaspoon salt
⅛ teaspoon freshly ground pepper
2 eggs, slightly beaten
1 cup milk
¾ cup French fried onions
1 tablespoon freshly snipped parsley for garnish (optional)
Paprika, for garnish (optional)

Preheat oven to 350°. Spray a 9" x 13" baking dish with nonstick spray coating. In a large skillet, sauté the onion and red pepper in butter over medium-low heat for about 10 to 15 minutes or until the onions are tender and lightly golden. Remove from heat. Add and blend in potatoes, cheese, olives, salt and pepper. Spoon into prepared baking pan. In a small bowl, beat together eggs and milk. Pour over onion mixture. Bake in preheated oven for 25 to 30 minutes or until heated through and golden. Remove from oven and sprinkle French onions over the top. Return to oven and bake for another 8 to 10 minutes or until the onions are toasted. To serve, sprinkle the parsley and a dash of paprika over the top, if desired.

Makes about 6 servings.

cottage fries

My mother made sure she always had plenty of cold, boiled potatoes on hand to prepare cottage fries for our family's hearty farm breakfasts. From her, I learned the secrets of thin slicing and low heat under a well-seasoned cast iron skillet to ensure their very best flavor.

3 tablespoons butter or margarine
6 medium cold, boiled potatoes
Salt and pepper to taste

In a 10-inch heavy cast iron skillet over medium-low heat, melt the butter. Carefully slice the potatoes as thin as possible into the melted butter. Sprinkle lightly with salt and pepper. Cook until potatoes are brown and crusty on all sides, for about 20 to 25 minutes; occasionally turn the potatoes using a wide spatula to keep the slices from breaking. Serve hot.

Makes about 6 servings.

Tips

- When preparing cottage fries, allow 1 large potato for each serving.

- Do not fry more than 1 pound of potato slices in a 10-inch skillet at a time. Most likely the slices will not fry evenly as some of them will steam and you will not get the nice crusty fries you're looking for.

turkey hash browns

Variations on the classic hash brown abound. Here is a version that not only goes together quickly, but has a great flavor.

2 tablespoons butter or margarine
3 cups diced, uncooked, peeled red-skinned or other waxy potatoes
1 cup chopped onion
1 cup diced green pepper
2 cups diced cooked turkey
½ cup chicken broth, divided
1 teaspoon salt
¼ teaspoon ground thyme
⅛ teaspoon freshly ground black pepper

In a 10-inch skillet, over medium-low heat, melt the butter. Add the potatoes, onion, and green pepper. Cook for 10 to 15 minutes, stirring occasionally. Stir in the turkey, ¼ cup broth, salt, thyme, and pepper. Stir to blend. Add more broth as needed, if the hash becomes dry. Continue cooking over low heat, gently stirring the mixture, for 10 to 15 minutes longer or until potatoes are well browned on both sides and tender. Serve warm.

Makes about 6 servings.

Variation

Beef Hash Browns
Replace the turkey in this recipe with diced, lean roast beef.

Thomas Jefferson gets the credit for introducing French fries to American fare when he served them at a White House dinner. John Adams thought Jefferson was putting on airs by serving "such novelties."

In 1993,
a 30-pound
potato was
grown in
Riyadh,
Saudi Arabia;
big enough to
make 150
servings of
French fries.

rosemary potato and garlic oven fries

You can boil the potatoes the night before to give yourself a jumpstart. Also, it's easier to slice the potatoes as thin as this recipe calls for if they're cold.

Nonstick spray coating
2 tablespoons minced garlic
1 teaspoon powdered rosemary or to taste
2 tablespoons olive oil
½ teaspoon salt
Freshly ground black pepper to taste
10 medium red potatoes, boiled until tender, cooled, peeled and thinly sliced
1 tablespoon snipped fresh chives, for garnish (optional)

Preheat oven to 400°. Spray a 9" x 13" baking pan with nonstick spray coating. In a small bowl, whisk together garlic, rosemary, and olive oil. Layer sliced potatoes, overlapping slightly on bottom of prepared baking dish. Drizzle oil mixture over the top. Sprinkle with salt and pepper. Bake in preheated oven for 30 to 45 minutes or until potatoes evenly browned and crisp. Serve garnished with snipped chives, if desired.

Makes about 6 servings.

roasted potato skins

These crispy skins, served plain or with your favorite seasonings or dips, make a terrific snack. They'll disappear quickly. Save the scooped-out potato portions to use in soup or shape into patties and fry in butter.

6 large russet potatoes, unpeeled, scrubbed, and dried
¼ cup butter OR 3 tablespoons olive oil
¼ teaspoon paprika
Pinch of pepper
Salt to taste
Optional seasonings:
    Sour cream and chives, salsa, guacamole, grated Parmesan cheese, shredded Cheddar cheese, grated Pepper Jack cheese or garlic salt.

Preheat the oven to 425°. Pierce the skins of each potato in several places with fork. Place potatoes in preheated oven directly on rack and bake for 45 to 60 minutes or until potatoes are fork tender. Let the potatoes cool at least two hours. The skins tend to tear if you prepare them when the potatoes are still warm. When the potatoes have cooled, cut each in half lengthwise. Scoop out the pulp, leaving a shell ¼-inch thick. Reserve the pulp for future use. Cut each potato skin in half lengthwise. When ready to serve increase oven temperature to 475°. Arrange skins, cut side up, on a large baking sheet. In a small saucepan, heat butter or olive oil. Whisk in paprika and pepper. Brush the insides of the potato skins with the butter mixture. Bake potato skins in preheated oven for 15 to 20 minutes or until the skins are well browned and crisp. Salt to taste. Serve the skins very hot with your favorite seasonings or dips.

Makes about 6 servings.

- Potato skins can be set aside and chilled until needed.

- Leftover roasted potato skins can be reheated in the microwave.

rosti potatoes

This recipe is inspired by the Swiss version of hash browns. Some refer to it as a potato pancake. No matter what you call it, the crispy crust and tender, oniony interior of rosti is full of down home flavor.

3 large Yukon Gold potatoes,
    about 1½ pounds, peeled
1 cup thinly sliced, well-washed leek
Coarse salt and freshly ground
    black pepper, to taste
5 to 6 tablespoons butter, divided

Grate the potatoes using a shredding disk on a food processor or the large holes of a box grater. Do not rinse. Toss into a mixing bowl with leek, salt, and pepper. Heat butter in a 10-inch cast iron skillet over medium-high heat. When the butter is sizzling, add the potatoes and press down gently with a large metal spatula to make a thin, level layer. Reduce the heat to medium-low. Cook until the bottom is golden brown and crusty, for about 5 minutes. Cover tightly, and continue to cook for another 5 minutes, shaking the pan from time to time so that the potatoes do not stick. Uncover, press down the top and gently slide the spatula around the edges to check on browning and to prevent sticking. Continue to cook for 5 to 6 minutes longer or until the bottom is nicely browned and the top is slightly dry. Cover the skillet with a flat plate. Invert the skillet, flipping the potato cake out onto the plate. Scrape out any stuck bits. Add remaining butter to the skillet. Carefully slide the rosti back into the skillet. Repeat the cooking method, adding more butter if necessary, for another 10 to 15 minutes or until the underside is crisp and golden. Serve immediately turned out onto a large heated plate and cut into wedges.

Makes about 6 servings.

easy oven fries

Oven fries provide the flavor of traditional French fries with only a fraction of the work and less oily, healthier result.

Nonstick spray coating
6 large russet potatoes, peeled
2 tablespoons olive oil
Coarse salt to taste
Optional Seasonings:
    Sour cream and snipped chives, salsa,
    guacamole, grated Parmesan cheese,
    shredded Cheddar cheese, shredded
    Pepper Jack cheese, or garlic salt.

Preheat oven to 475°. Spray a large cookie sheet with nonstick spray coating. Cut potatoes into ¼-inch thick strips. Place in ice cold water to rinse. Drain. Spread on towel and pat dry. In a large bowl, toss potatoes and olive oil. Spread potatoes out on prepared cookie sheet. Bake for about 20 minutes. Remove from oven and turn potatoes. Bake for 15 to 20 minutes more or until potatoes are browned and tender. Remove from oven. Sprinkle with salt. Serve warm.

Makes about 4 servings.

Variations

- Before baking, sprinkle potatoes with 1 tablespoon finely snipped parsley, ½ teaspoon freshly ground black pepper, and ¼ teaspoon garlic powder.

- Before baking, sprinkle potatoes with 2 teaspoons paprika, 1 teaspoon onion powder, and ½ teaspoon salt.

- Before baking, sprinkle potatoes with your favorite dry seasoning mix such as Creole seasoning, ranch, Italian, or dry onion soup mix.

A traditional Cornish dish is "tattie fry" or potato "jowdie." It's made by filling a pan with sliced raw spuds, chopped onion, salt, and pepper. Water to cover is added and the pan is covered until the ingredients are tender. Cornish cooks sometimes serve tattie fry with eggs on top.

assorted dips for roasted potato skins and oven fries

If you're looking for some imaginative ways beyond catsup to add heat and zip to your oven fries and roasted potato skins, I suggest the following dip recipes.

creamy mustard dip

2 cups sour cream
¼ cup country style Dijon mustard
¼ teaspoon garlic powder
2 teaspoons white wine vinegar

In a medium bowl, combine all ingredients. Chill. Serve as a dipping sauce for oven fries or roasted potato skins.

Makes about 1¼ cups.

hot and spicy dip

1 cup cottage cheese
¼ cup milk
3 tablespoons chopped, canned green chiles
1 tablespoon creamy peanut butter
½ teaspoon onion powder
¼ teaspoon ginger
¼ teaspoon salt

In a blender, combine all ingredients. Cover and process until smooth. Chill several hours or overnight to blend flavors. Serve as a dipping sauce for oven fries or roasted potato skins.

Makes about 1½ cups.

hot horseradish dip

2 cups sour cream
3 tablespoons prepared horseradish
½ teaspoon hot pepper sauce
¼ teaspoon salt

In a medium bowl, combine all ingredients. Cover. Chill until ready to serve.

Makes about 2 cups.

sombrero dip

2 cups cottage cheese
1 cup plain yogurt
½ cup finely chopped red onion
2-2½ teaspoons ground cumin
¾ teaspoon hot pepper sauce

In a medium bowl, combine all ingredients. Cover and chill several hours to blend flavors. Serve as a dipping sauce for oven fries or roasted potato skins.

Makes about 3½ cups.

red ranch dip

1 cup ketchup
¾ cup ranch-style dressing

In a small bowl, combine ketchup and dressing. Cover and chill until ready to serve. Serve as a dipping sauce for oven fries or roasted potato skins.

Makes about 1¾ cups.

Tips

- For a spicy taste change, blend grated Parmesan cheese, salt, spicy chili powder, and red cayenne pepper, then shake over homemade fries.

- Potatoes are great roasted alone, with other vegetables, or alongside a roast. Simply cut potatoes to desired size, toss with a little olive oil, add seasonings, roast and enjoy.

Bleu 'n Brie potato casserole

This easy-to-prepare casserole, featuring the sophisticated flavors of Brie and Bleu cheese, makes it a dish to remember.

4 medium potatoes, washed and peeled
Nonstick spray coating
8 ounces Brie cheese
I cup plain yogurt
2 eggs
1 tablespoon snipped parsley
Salt and pepper to taste
4 tablespoons butter, melted
1 cup crumbled Bleu cheese
Paprika for garnish (optional)

In a large saucepan, cook potatoes in boiling water until tender. Drain and dice. Meanwhile, preheat oven to 350°. Spray a 1½ quart shallow casserole with nonstick spray coating. Spoon potatoes into casserole. In a blender or food processor, combine Brie cheese, yogurt, eggs, parsley, salt, and pepper. Process until smooth. Pour over diced potatoes. Stir to mix well. Press down to even out. Drizzle with melted butter. Bake in preheated oven for 30 to 35 minutes or until heated through and golden. Sprinkle crumbled Bleu cheese on top the last 10 minutes of baking. To serve, sprinkle with a dash of paprika, if desired.

Makes about 4 servings.

casseroles and gratins

A simple yet sumptuous assortment of casserole and gratin recipes for the next time you're looking for a one-dish meal.

beef-Cheddar potato scallop

If you like tomatoes, cheese, and hamburger with your potatoes, then you'll like this tasty casserole.

1 (14½-ounce) can stewed tomatoes
1 teaspoon grated orange rind
1 teaspoon salt
1 teaspoon dried sweet basil
¼ teaspoon freshly ground pepper
4-5 medium potatoes (1½ pound)
    sliced ⅛-inch thick
1 pound lean ground beef,
    broken into small pieces
1½ cups grated sharp Cheddar cheese,
    divided
Orange wedges
Snipped parsley

In a shallow, 2-quart microwave dish, mix tomatoes, orange rind, salt, basil and pepper. Add potatoes, mix and spread in an even layer. Cover loosely with plastic wrap. Microwave on high power 8 minutes. Stir. Cover and microwave on high for 8 minutes more. Stir in beef and ½ cup of cheese. Cover and microwave on high for 10 minutes. Stir. Cover with remaining cheese. Microwave, uncovered, on high for for 5 to 8 minutes or until potatoes are just tender. Let stand 5 minutes. Garnish with orange wedges and chopped parsley.

Makes about 6 servings.

coconut and sweet potato casserole

Pretty as a picture and not too sweet, this is an outstanding yet simple-to-prepare dish. Serve it as a special holiday meal with roast turkey or ham.

Nonstick spray coating
3 medium sweet potatoes,
    unpeeled, cooked and cooled
⅓ cup brown sugar, firmly packed
½ cup hot water
¼ teaspoon salt
3 tablespoons butter or margarine
⅓ cup sweetened flake coconut
Whole maraschino cherries, without stems,
    for garnish (optional)

Preheat heat oven to 350°. Spray a 9" plate or shallow baking pan with nonstick spray coating. Set aside. Peel sweet potatoes and cut in ½-inch slices. Arrange slices in prepared baking pan. In a small bowl combine sugar, hot water, salt, and butter. Pour over sweet potatoes. Bake in preheated oven for 25 minutes, basting occasionally with the syrup. Sprinkle top with coconut and bake for 15 minutes longer or until coconut is lightly browned. Serve warm. Garnish with maraschino cherries, if desired.

Makes about 4 servings.

greek potato-lamb casserole with green beans

This one-dish dinner also reheats well.

¾ pound lean lamb, trimmed of all fat
  and cut in ¾-inch pieces
1 cup plain yogurt
2 garlic cloves, crushed
2 teaspoons sweet paprika
1 teaspoon grated fresh ginger
½-1 teaspoon salt, to taste
¼ teaspoon freshly ground black pepper
  to taste
1 tablespoon olive oil
1 medium onion, chopped
2 medium tomatoes, chopped
2 medium Yukon Gold potatoes,
  peeled and cut in 1-inch cubes
¼ pound fresh green beans,
  trimmed and halved crosswise
½ cup pitted and sliced black olives

In a medium bowl, combine and stir lamb, yogurt, garlic, paprika, ginger, salt and pepper until well mixed. Cover and refrigerate for 2 to 4 hours. Preheat oven to 350°. In a medium Dutch oven, heat olive oil. Add onion and tomatoes. Sauté over medium-high heat until vegetables are soft, for 10 minutes, stirring often. Spoon mixture over lamb, stirring to combine (to help prevent yogurt from curdling during cooking). Turn lamb mixture back into the Dutch oven. Add potatoes and green beans. Cover and bring casserole to just a slow boil. Transfer pot to preheated oven. Bake until lamb and potatoes are tender, about 45 to 50 minutes. Serve warm, topped with sliced black olives.

Makes about 4 servings.

swiss potato 'n ham casserole

The Swiss cheese in the sauce makes this colorful dish smooth and creamy.

Nonstick spray coating
6 medium Yukon Gold potatoes,
  peeled and cubed
3 cups cubed ham
2 tablespoons butter
1 cup minced onion
½ cup diced green pepper
½ cup diced sweet red pepper
2 tablespoons flour
1 teaspoon salt
¼ teaspoon freshly ground pepper
2 cups milk
2 cups shredded Swiss cheese
3 tablespoons snipped chives

Preheat oven to 350°. Spray a 3-quart casserole or baking pan with nonstick spray coating and set aside. In medium saucepan, cook potatoes in boiling water to cover until just tender. Drain. Place potatoes and ham in prepared casserole. In a large heavy skillet over low heat, melt the butter. Add the onion and peppers. Cook, stirring occasionally, until tender for about 5 to 7 minutes. Whisk in the flour, salt, and pepper. Cook, stirring constantly, for 3 minutes. Do not brown. Pour in the milk all at once, whisking constantly until smooth. Simmer gently over low heat until thick, for 3 to 5 minutes. Stir in cheese until melted, 2 to 3 minutes. Pour mixture over potatoes and ham. Stir gently to coat all ingredients. Bake for 40 to 45 minutes or until bubbly and top is lightly browned. Just before serving, sprinkle chives over the top.

Makes about 8 servings.

caraway cheese potatoes

Here is a party-size recipe for scalloped potatoes that is a real crowd pleaser, especially when served with ham.

Nonstick spray coating
¼ cup butter
3 tablespoons all-purpose flour
1½ teaspoons caraway seeds*
1 teaspoon salt
¼ teaspoon pepper
3 cups milk
6 large red potatoes (about 3 pounds) peeled and thinly sliced
2 medium onions, thinly sliced
2 cups shredded sharp Cheddar cheese
2 teaspoons snipped chives, for garnish (optional)

Preheat oven to 350°. Spray a 3-quart baking dish with nonstick spray coating. In a medium saucepan, melt butter over medium heat. Stir in flour, caraway seeds, salt, and pepper. Blend until smooth. Gradually stir in milk. Bring to a boil, stirring constantly. Boil and stir for 1 minute. Remove from heat. Arrange potatoes and onions in prepared baking dish. Pour sauce over the top. Cover and bake for 1 hour. Remove cover. Bake for an additional 30 minutes or until potatoes are tender. Sprinkle cheese over the top during the last 10 minutes of baking.

Makes about 12 servings.

*Tip
To obtain the best flavor from caraway seeds, crush them with the flat side of a large knife or with the back of a spoon before adding them to whatever dish you are preparing.

salmon potato strata

This easy one-dish dinner brings color, taste, and a refreshing change of pace to the dinner table.

Nonstick spray coating
1 can (15½ ounces) salmon, drained and flaked
1 medium onion, chopped (½ cup)
½ cup diced celery
¼ cup diced green pepper
¼ cup diced sweet red pepper
4 eggs, slightly beaten
2 cups milk
1½ teaspoons salt, divided
¼ teaspoon dried dillweed
⅛ teaspoon pepper
4 medium red potatoes (6 cups unpeeled and cut into ⅛-inch slices)
¾ cup canned French fried onions, for garnish (optional)

Preheat oven to 350°. Spray a 1½-quart casserole or baking pan with nonstick spray coating. In a large bowl, combine salmon, onion, celery, green and red peppers, eggs, milk, ½ teaspoon salt, dillweed and pepper. Mix thoroughly. Place half of potatoes in prepared casserole. Sprinkle with ½ teaspoon salt and spread half of salmon mixture over potatoes. Repeat with remaining potatoes, salt, and salmon. Bake in preheated oven for I hour and 20 minutes or until potatoes test tender when pierced with a fork. Remove from oven and sprinkle French fried onions over the top. Return to oven and continue baking until onions are toasted. Remove from oven and let stand for 5 minutes before serving.

Makes about 8 servings.

florentine potato puff

A square of this hearty gratin is wonderful served with grilled chops of any kind.

Nonstick spray coating
3 cups mashed potatoes
1½ cups (12 ounces)
    cream-style cottage cheese
4 eggs, separated
1 package (10 ounces) frozen chopped
    spinach, thawed and drained
½ cup freshly grated Parmesan cheese
⅓ cup minced onion
1½ teaspoons salt
¼ teaspoon pepper
⅛ teaspoon nutmeg
2 tablespoons roasted garlic bread crumbs

Preheat oven to 375°. Spray a 3-quart deep baking dish with nonstick spray coating. In a large mixing bowl, combine potatoes, cottage cheese, egg yolks, spinach, Parmesan cheese, onion, salt, pepper, and nutmeg. Beat until well blended. In a small mixing bowl, beat egg whites until stiff peaks form. Fold into potato mixture. Turn into prepared casserole. Sprinkle breadcrumbs over the top. Bake in preheated oven for 1 hour or until knife inserted in center of puff comes out clean.

Makes about 6 servings.

french potato-garlic gratin

Here is an easy way to dress up potatoes for a family or company dinner. The lightly salted, nutty flavor of grated Gruyere cheese lends an exquisite taste to the humble potato gratin.

1 large clove garlic, smashed
3 tablespoons butter, divided
4 medium potatoes,
    peeled and thinly sliced
Salt and pepper to taste
Freshly grated nutmeg
1 egg, slightly beaten
½ cup milk
1 cup shredded Gruyere cheese

Preheat oven to 350°. Rub the inside of a shallow earthen casserole with the smashed garlic. Mince the leftover portion. Generously spread butter over the bottom of the casserole. Layer the potato slices over the butter. Scatter the minced garlic across the potatoes. Sprinkle with salt, pepper, and a pinch of freshly grated nutmeg. In a small bowl, beat the egg and milk until blended. Pour over the potatoes. Sprinkle the grated cheese over the top. Dot with remaining butter. Bake in preheated oven for 40 to 45 minutes or until the top is golden and potatoes are tender.

Makes about 4 servings.

"The potatoes never failed us. For each meal they looked different and tasted different."
– Yuri Sahl, from One Foot in America

basil potato-vegetable

Just spoon the vegetables over the mashed potato base for this attractive and easy-to-prepare oven dish.

Nonstick spray coating
1 large egg, slightly beaten
¼ cup milk
1½ teaspoon salt, divided
¼ cup grated Parmesan cheese
2 cups mashed potatoes
1 tablespoon olive or vegetable oil
1 medium onion,
    halved and sliced crosswise (1 cup)
1 small sweet red pepper, chopped (1 cup)
1 medium zucchini, halved lengthwise and
    cut in ½-inch slices (2 cups)
1 tablespoon snipped fresh basil
½ teaspoon salt
1 tablespoon toasted breadcrumbs
Parsley, for garnish (optional)

Preheat oven to 450°. Spray a 9" pie plate with nonstick spray coating. In a medium mixing bowl, combine egg, milk, salt, and cheese with potatoes. Turn potatoes into prepared pie plate and press the mixture with the back of large spoon or rubber spatula evenly over the bottom. In a large skillet, heat the oil over medium-high heat. Add onion and cook, stirring occasionally, until golden, for about 8 minutes. Add the red pepper, zucchini, and remaining salt. Continue cooking, stirring occasionally, until crisp tender, for about 10 minutes. Stir in basil and salt. Spoon the mixture into the middle of the mashed potatoes, leaving a 2-inch border of potatoes uncovered. (Vegetables will settle during baking.) Sprinkle breadcrumbs over all. Bake in preheated oven for 15 to 20 minutes or until potatoes are puffed and golden. Serve warm, sprinkled with parsley, if desired.

Makes about 4 servings.

golden shepherd's pie

Potatoes are basic to Shepherd's pie. I believe it's one of the world's greatest dishes to make with leftovers. The British claim credit for creating this dish, using leftover lamb roast. It also tastes great with leftover roast pork, veal, and as I have used here, beef.

2 tablespoons butter
1 cup finely chopped onions
½ cup diced carrots
½ cup diced celery
2 tablespoons finely snipped parsley
3 tablespoons flour
2 tablespoons tomato paste
2 cups of chicken broth
1 teaspoon Worcestershire sauce
Freshly ground pepper to taste
3 cups cooked, cubed, very lean roast beef
1 cup cooked peas
3-3½ cups mashed potatoes
1 cup shredded sharp Cheddar cheese
Paprika for garnish (optional)

Preheat oven to 350°. In a large saucepan, heat the butter. Add onions, carrots, celery, and parsley. Cook, stirring, until the onions are wilted. Sprinkle and whisk in the flour over the onion mixture. Add tomato paste, broth, Worcestershire, and pepper. Continue to whisk until blended and thickened. Let simmer for 10 minutes. Stir in diced meat and peas. Cook for 5 minutes longer. Pour the mixture into a 3-quart baking dish or casserole. Spoon the mashed potatoes over the top of the mixture. Place the dish in the preheated oven. Bake for 35 to 45 minutes or until heated through. Sprinkle the cheese evenly on the top before the last 10 minutes of baking. Allow the cheese to melt and lightly brown. Remove from oven and sprinkle with a dash of paprika, if desired.

Makes about 6 servings.

Asiago and potato-egg gratin

The mellow nutty flavor of Asiago cheese is a perfect complement to both potatoes and eggs. The combination creates a savory gratin with a creamy, almost molten interior under a crispy crust. Serve it with your favorite beef, pork, or lamb roast and a simple vegetable blend such as peas and carrots.

4 medium russet potatoes (1½ pounds)
Nonstick spray coating.
1 tablespoon butter or margarine
¼ cup diced onions
1½ teaspoons finely chopped garlic
3 tablespoons flour
½ cup light cream
1 cup sour cream
1 cup grated Asiago cheese
2 tablespoons snipped parsley
1 teaspoon salt
½ teaspoon paprika
⅛ teaspoon pepper
4 hard-cooked eggs, sliced
4 plum tomatoes, cut in wedges
1 cup soft bread crumbs
2 tablespoon olive oil
Parsley, for garnish, (optional)

In a large saucepan, cook potatoes in boiling water until tender. Drain. Peel and thinly slice. Meanwhile, preheat oven to 350°. Spray a 1½-quart shallow casserole with nonstick spray coating. In a large saucepan, melt butter over medium heat. Add onion and garlic and cook until onions are wilted and tender. Do not brown. Blend in flour. Gradually stir in light cream until smooth. Stir sour cream, cheese, parsley, salt, paprika and pepper. Cook and stir over low heat until cheese is melted and blended into the mixture. Stir in potatoes. Spread half the mixture into prepared casserole. Top with egg slices and tomato wedges. Spoon remaining potato mixture over the top. Press down to even out. In a small bowl, toss breadcrumbs with olive oil and sprinkle over the potatoes. Press down to even out. Bake in preheated oven for 35 to 40 minutes or until potatoes are heated through and top is golden. To serve, lightly sprinkle with parsley if desired.

Makes about 6 servings.

jansson's temptation

A tasty casserole of potatoes, anchovies and cream—crisp and brown on top, rich and creamy within.

6 medium potatoes
Nonstick spray coating
5 tablespoons butter, divided
1½ cups thinly sliced onions
2 (2-ounce) cans flat anchovy fillets, drained*
Freshly ground black pepper, to taste
2 tablespoons of bread crumbs
¾ cup half and half
Snipped fresh parsley (optional)

Peel potatoes and cut into 2" x ½" strips, and place in water. Preheat oven to 400°. Spray a 2-quart casserole with nonstick spray coating. Set aside.

In a medium skillet, melt 2 tablespoons butter and add onions. Cook until soft, but not browned. Drain potatoes and pat dry. In prepared casserole, arrange a layer of potatoes using about one-third the total amount. Arrange 1 can of the anchovy fillets and half the onions over the potatoes. Season with pepper. Repeat with remaining ingredients, ending with a layer of potatoes. Dot with and scatter the remaining butter. Sprinkle with pepper and breadcrumbs. Pour half-and-half over all. Bake in preheated oven, uncovered, until the potatoes are well cooked and very tender and have absorbed all the cream, for about 45 to 60 minutes. Serve warm with a dusting of parsley, if desired.

Makes about 6 servings.

*Note:
If desired, soak the anchovies in water or milk for 5 minutes to reduce the saltiness.

The legend of Jansson's Temptation

It is claimed Erik Jansson, a Swedish religious zealot, couldn't be tempted. Emigrating to America from his native land, he renounced all worldly pleasure. He did, however, have a taste for this aromatic concoction. Legend has it that one day, his followers discovered Jansson in hiding, devouring a large bowl of this delectable dish.

Tip
A New Twist on an Old Favorite

Try this zesty twist to make an everyday casserole new again: Mix the crumbs from your last bag of potato chips with a little grated cheese. Sprinkle generously on top of the casserole after it's done, then pop it under the broiler for a few minutes to melt the cheese and serve.

Overview

The following recipes have been tested using russet potatoes, which I consider the ideal potato for baking. It's the most floury and the least moist, two qualities important when bread making. Usually two to three potatoes will produce two cups of riced potatoes. If you don't have a ricer, a potato masher works fine; just be certain there are no lumps.

Adding mashed potatoes along with some of the water in which they're cooked gives the bread a finer texture. The result is baked goods that are light but not dry, with the irresistible, earthy flavor blend of yeasted wheat and potato.

For convenience, you can simplify most of these recipes by using packaged, instant mashed potatoes for the fresh potatoes, eliminating much work. Follow package directions, since yields vary between buds, flakes and different brands. Substitute warm water for any cooking water called for.

For all my recipe testing, I used quick-rising active dry yeast, because it's readily available and I know most cooks favor its convenience. Compressed or regular active dry yeast may be substituted.

I make bread in a heavy-duty mixer and use a strong wooden spoon for any stirring. As for kneading, strong arms are required, but the end results are worth the effort.

If these breads don't start your mouth watering, you're just not temptable. Like other home-baked breads, potato breads are loaded with goodness and flavor, but these have special variations that make them truly delicious.

breads, rolls, muffins, and scones

If you're one of the many cooks who treasure memories of plump, richly browned potato bread, you'll recognize some of the following recipes. If you've never baked or sampled potato bread and its fresh-from-the-oven goodness, now may be the time.

potato bread

This is a very good recipe to have on hand and use often. It not only tastes great right from the oven, and makes tasty toast, but it also freezes well.

1 medium potato,
   peeled and coarsely chopped
1 package active dry yeast
2 tablespoons butter
2 tablespoons sugar
1 teaspoon salt
1 cup milk
5-5½ cups all-purpose flour
Nonstick spray coating

In a medium saucepan, cook potato in boiling water until tender, for 15 to 20 minutes. Drain, reserving ¾ cup potato water. Pour reserved potato liquid into large mixer bowl. Let cool to 120-130°. Sprinkle yeast over warm liquid. Let stand until softened. In a large bowl, combine potatoes, butter, sugar, salt, and 2 tablespoons of milk. Beat with an electric mixer or mash until smoothly puréed. Gradually beat in remaining milk. Stir into liquid mixture. Add 3 cups flour. Mix at low speed to blend, then beat at medium speed until smooth and elastic (for about 5 minutes).

With a wooden spoon, stir in about 1½ cups additional flour to make a soft dough. Turn out onto work surface coated with 1 to 1½ cups flour. Knead until dough is smooth and elastic (for about 8 to 10 minutes), adding only enough flour to prevent dough from becoming sticky. Spray a large bowl with nonstick spray coating. Place dough in bowl and turn once to coat both sides. Cover and let rise until doubled in bulk (for about 1 hour). Punch dough down and divide into 2 equal portions. Cover and let rest for 5 minutes. Spray two 4½" x 8½" loaf pans with nonstick spray coating. Shape each dough portion into a loaf and place into a prepared pan. Dust lightly with a little flour. Cover and let rise until almost doubled (for about 45 minutes). Preheat oven to 375°. Bake loaves until well browned; they should sound hollow when you tap them with a finger (for about 35 to 40 minutes). Remove loaves from pan and let cool on wire racks.

Makes 2 loaves.

Potato Bread Tips

- To enjoy potato bread, rolls, biscuits, and muffins at their best, eat them when they are still warm from the oven.

- Dusting corn meal inside greased pans gives the crust an interesting texture.

- When slashing or scoring the tops of loaves, use care not to drive out the air and flatten the loaf. Make shallow cuts with a very sharp knife.

- For shiny crisp crusts, brush potato bread or rolls before baking with 1 egg yolk beaten into 2 tablespoons cold water.

- For soft golden crusts, brush potato breads or rolls right after baking with melted butter.

potato egg bread

This recipe makes two large, handsome, round loaves for everyday or party use. Superb fresh from the oven slathered with butter and your favorite spread, or toasted the next day.

7 1/2-8 cups all-purpose flour
2 tablespoons sugar
4 teaspoons salt
2 packages active dry yeast
1/2 cup water
1 1/2 cups mashed potatoes
1 1/2 cups milk
1/4 cup butter or margarine
2 eggs
Nonstick spray coating

In a large mixing bowl, combine 1 1/2 cups flour, sugar, salt, and yeast. In a 2-quart saucepan, mix water, mashed potatoes, milk, and butter and heat until warm (120°-130°). Add potato mixture to flour mixture. With mixer at low speed, gradually blend liquid into dry ingredients. Beat in eggs. Increase speed to medium and beat for 2 minutes, occasionally scraping bowl. Beat in 1 cup flour to make a thick batter and continue beating for an additional 2 minutes, scraping bowl often. Using a wooden spoon, stir in enough additional flour (about 3 1/2 cups) to make a soft dough. Turn dough out onto a lightly floured surface and knead in enough of the flour (about 1 1/2 cups) to make a moderately soft dough that is smooth and elastic (for 8 to 10 minutes total). Shape the dough into a ball. Spray a large bowl with nonstick spray coating. Place dough in bowl, turning once to coat the surface of the dough. Cover and let rise in a warm place until double in size (for about 1 hour). Punch dough down.

Turn dough out onto lightly floured surface. Divide dough in half and shape each into a round ball. Cover with a towel and let rest 15 minutes. Spray two 1 1/2 quart, round, shallow casseroles with nonstick spray coating. Place dough in prepared casseroles. Slash an "X" on top of each. Cover and let rise until nearly double in size (for about 1 hour). Preheat oven to 400°. Bake for 40 minutes or until well browned. The bread should sound hollow when you tap the top with your fingers. Remove from casseroles immediately. Brush the top with soft butter. Cool on racks.

Makes two 2 1/4-pound loaves.

pumpernickel bread

Flavorful pumpernickel—a moist and hearty, deep-brown bread first made in fifteenth century Germany—is an ideal choice for home baking, and excellent for cheese sandwiches.

8 cups all-purpose flour
3 cups rye flour
2 tablespoons salt
1 cup wheat bran
1 cup yellow corn meal, divided
2 packages active dry yeast
3½ cups water
¼ cup dark molasses
2 squares (1 ounce each)
   unsweetened chocolate
2 tablespoons butter
3 teaspoons instant coffee
2 cups mashed potatoes
   (room temperature)
2 tablespoons caraway seeds
Nonstick spray coating

In a large bowl, combine all-purpose flour and rye flour. In a large mixing bowl, combine 2 cups of flour mixture, salt, bran, ¾ cup corn meal, and yeast. In a medium saucepan combine water, molasses, chocolate, butter, and instant coffee. Heat over low heat until liquids are very warm (120 -130°). Gradually add to flour mixture and beat for 2 minutes at medium speed of electric mixer, scraping bowl occasionally.

Add potatoes and 1 cup flour. Beat at high speed for 2 minutes, scraping bowl occasionally. Using a wooden spoon, stir in caraway seeds and as much of the flour mixture as possible. Turn out onto a lightly floured surface. Cover and let rest for 15 minutes. Knead in enough of the remaining flour to make a moderately soft dough that is smooth and elastic, about 15 minutes. Spray a large bowl with nonstick spray coating. Place dough in bowl, turning once to coat the surface of the dough. Cover and let rise in a warm place until double in size. Punch down and let rise again until almost doubled (for about 30 minutes). Punch dough down and turn out onto lightly floured surface.

Divide dough into 3 equal pieces. Shape into round balls. Spray three 9" or 10" pie pans with nonstick spray coating. Sprinkle remaining corn meal over the spray coating. Place shaped dough in prepared pans. Cover and let rise in warm place until nearly double in size, for about 45 minutes. Preheat oven to 350°. Bake for about 50 minutes or until bread sounds hollow when tapped with your finger. Remove from oven and cool on wire racks.

Makes 3 round loaves.

Note
For a crisp crust, brush top of loaves with cold water just before baking. For a tender crust, brush with melted butter before baking.

Cheddar cheese potato bread

The mouthwatering aroma wafting from your oven when this bread is baking will tempt your family to treat themselves to the old-fashioned goodness of a still-warm, fresh-baked slice of bread. The bite of the coarse ground pepper adds a nippy flavor.

5-5½ cups all-purpose flour
2 packages active dry yeast
1 cup milk
⅔ cup butter, cut up
1 tablespoon sugar
2 to 3 tablespoons fresh coarse
   ground pepper, to taste
1 teaspoon salt
4 eggs
2 cups shredded sharp Cheddar cheese
1½ cups mashed potatoes
Nonstick spray coating

In a large mixing bowl, combine 2 cups flour and yeast. In a small saucepan, combine the milk, butter, sugar, 2 tablespoons pepper (or to taste) and salt. Heat and stir over moderate heat until warm (120 to 130°) and butter is melted. Add to flour mixture. Add eggs and beat with an electric mixer on low speed until blended, for about 30 seconds. Scrape down sides of bowl. Beat at high speed for 3 minutes. With a wooden spoon, stir in Cheddar cheese, potatoes, and as much remaining flour as possible. Turn out onto a lightly floured surface. Knead in enough remaining flour to make a moderately stiff dough that is smooth and elastic (for 6 to 8 minutes). Spray a large bowl with nonstick spray coating. Shape dough into ball.

Place dough in prepared bowl, turning once to coat both sides. Cover and allow to rise in a warm place until doubled (about 1 hour). Spray 2 large cookie sheets with nonstick spray coating. Set aside. Punch down and turn dough out onto a lightly floured surface. Divide dough into six equal pieces. Cover and let rest for 10 minutes. Roll each piece into a 16-inch rope. On a prepared cookie sheet, braid three ropes together. Repeat on second prepared sheet with remaining ropes. Cover and let rise in a warm place until nearly doubled (for about 30 minutes). Preheat oven to 375°. Bake braids for 40 to 45 minutes or until well browned; they should sound hollow when tapped with a finger. If over-browning occurs, cover with foil for the last 15 minutes of baking. Remove from pans and cool on wire racks.

Makes two braids.

Potato Product Usage

According to the records of the National Potato Board, the following percentages of potatoes of all varieties were used in the year 2000:

Fresh market   26%
Frozen products   35%
Potato chips   10%
Dehydrated products   11%
Canned products   1%

french twist potato bread

A thick, flat bread, creamy-textured and moist. This bread's flavor is unbeatable, especially when served warm and fresh from the oven with a robust soup.

1 large russet potato, peeled and cubed
1 cup water
5½-6 cups all-purpose flour
2 packages active dry yeast
1 teaspoon salt
1 egg white, slightly beaten
1 tablespoon water
Nonstick spray coating
1 tablespoon coarse-grained salt
1 teaspoon coarsely ground black pepper
Cornmeal

In a saucepan, combine potato cubes and 1 cup water. Bring to a boil. Reduce heat. Cover and simmer until potatoes are fork tender, about 15 minutes. Remove from heat. Mash potatoes in the liquid. Measure the mixture and blend in additional water to make 2 cups. Cool the potato mixture to 120-130°. In a large mixing bowl, combine 1½ cups flour, yeast, salt, and potato mixture. Beat on low speed to blend ingredients. Continue beating on high speed for 3 minutes, stopping occasionally to scrape the bowl. Using a wooden spoon, stir in as much of the remaining flour as possible. Turn the dough onto a floured surface and knead 8-10 minutes or until the dough is smooth and elastic. Spray a large bowl with nonstick spray coating. Place dough in bowl, turning dough once to coat surface of the dough. Cover and let rise in warm place until double in size (for about 1 hour).

Punch dough down and turn out onto a lightly floured surface. Cut into 4 equal pieces. Cover and let rest for 5 minutes. In a small bowl, combine egg white and water, beating lightly until foamy. Spray two baking sheets with nonstick spray coating, sprinkle each with cornmeal. Roll each piece of dough into a 12- to 14-inch rope. Brush each with the egg-water mixture. Sprinkle lightly with coarse salt and black pepper. For each loaf, twist two of the ropes together to form one loaf. Place loaves on prepared baking sheets. Cover and let rise in warm place until nearly doubled in size, for about 35-40 minutes. Preheat oven to 375°. Bake for 35 to 40 minutes or until loaves are lightly browned and sound hollow when you tap the tops with your finger. Remove from baking sheets. Cool on wire racks.

Makes 2 loaves.

potato rolls

New Englanders called these light and tender rolls "featherbeds." Save the water when you boil the potatoes and use it to make these delicately flavored rolls.

7 ½-8 cups all-purpose flour
1 package active dry yeast
2 large potatoes, peeled and quartered
5 tablespoons butter, melted and divided
2 tablespoons sugar
1 ½ teaspoons salt
1 ½ cups potato water
¾ cup warm milk (110 to 115°)
Nonstick spray coating

Mix 4 cups flour and yeast and set aside. In a medium saucepan cook potatoes in water to cover, until tender. Drain and reserve water. In a large mixing bowl, mash potatoes. Blend in 3 tablespoons butter, sugar, and salt. Add potato water and milk. Cool to 110 to 115°. Stir in flour and yeast mixture, beating well.

Then add enough remaining flour to make dough stiff enough to knead. Turn dough out onto a lightly floured surface. Knead until smooth and elastic, for about 8 to 10 minutes. Form dough into ball.

Spray a large bowl with nonstick spray coating. Place dough in bowl and brush top with melted butter. Cover and let rise until doubled, or for 1 hour. Spray 2 baking sheets with nonstick spray coating. Turn dough out onto lightly floured surface. Pat out to ½-inch thickness. Cut and form by hand into 36 rolls. Place on prepared baking sheets, leaving space for spreading. Brush tops with melted butter and dust lightly with flour. Cover and let rise until double in size (for about 30 to 40 minutes). Heat oven to 400°. Bake in preheated oven for 20 minutes or until lightly browned.

Makes about 36 rolls.

potato batter buns

There's no need for time-consuming rolling and shaping, just drop the batter into muffin cups! Serve warm from the oven.

1 medium potato, peeled and cubed
1¼ cups water
1½ cups whole wheat flour
1¼ cups all-purpose flour
1 package active dry yeast
¼ cup sugar
2 tablespoons grated orange rind
2 teaspoons salt
¼ cup cooking oil
¼ cup sugar
¾ teaspoon cinnamon
Nonstick spray coating

In saucepan, cook potato, covered, in 1¼ cups water for 15 minutes or until tender. Do not drain. Mash potato in cooking liquid. Add enough additional water to make 1½ cups potato mixture. Cool to 120-130°. In large mixing bowl, combine the whole-wheat flour, ¼ cup of the all-purpose flour, yeast, sugar, orange rind, and salt. With mixer at low speed, gradually beat the potato mixture and oil into the dry ingredients just until blended. Increase speed to high and beat for 3 minutes, scraping sides of bowl occasionally. Use a wooden spoon to stir in remaining flour. Cover and let rise in warm place until double in size, for about 1 hour. Spray twelve 2½-inch muffin cups with nonstick spray coating. Set aside. Preheat oven to 400°. Stir down batter and let rest for 5 minutes. Divide batter into prepared muffin cups. Combine sugar and cinnamon and sprinkle lightly over the muffins. Cover and let rise until nearly double in size, for about 30 minutes. Bake in preheated oven for 18 minutes or until done. Remove from pans and cool on wire racks.

Makes 12 buns.

potato scallion biscuits

Old-fashioned biscuits are as tasty today as they were in years gone by, especially when served fresh from the oven with chutney or marmalade.

Nonstick spray coating
2 cups all-purpose flour
2½ teaspoons baking powder
1 teaspoon salt
¼ teaspoon baking soda
1 cup mashed potatoes
⅓ cup plus 2 teaspoons shortening
¾ cup buttermilk
½ cup minced scallions

Preheat oven to 450°. Spray a large baking sheet with nonstick spray coating and lightly flour. Set aside. In a large mixing bowl, combine flour, baking powder, salt and baking soda. Cut in potatoes and shortening with a pastry blender or 2 knives until crumbly. Add buttermilk and scallions, stirring until just moistened. Turn dough out onto lightly floured surface. Roll or pat out until ¾-inch thick. Cut with a 2-inch round biscuit cutter. Gather the dough trimmings and reroll. Cut out additional biscuits. Place the biscuits 1 inch apart on prepared baking sheet. Bake for 12 to 15 minutes or until golden. Serve warm or cooled.

Makes about 16 biscuits.

spicy apple muffins

These tasty moist muffins are good for breakfast or a snack.

Nonstick spray coating
1 cup buttermilk
¼ cup vegetable oil
¾ cup sugar
2 eggs, beaten
2 cups all-purpose flour
1½ teaspoon baking powder
1½ teaspoon baking soda
½ teaspoon salt
½ teaspoon ground cinnamon
⅛ teaspoon ground nutmeg
1 cup mashed potatoes
1 cup diced tart cooking apple

Preheat oven to 400°. Spray muffin pan cups with nonstick spray coating. Set aside. In a large mixing bowl, combine buttermilk, oil, sugar and eggs. Mix well. Combine flour, baking powder, baking soda, salt, cinnamon, and nutmeg. Toss together potatoes and apples. Add to flour mixture and stir lightly until other mixture is moistened (batter should be lumpy). Spoon batter into prepared muffin cups. Bake for 15 to 20 minutes or until golden brown.

Makes 18 muffins.

crisp potato fingers

The dough for these bite-sized appetizers can be prepared ahead and kept chilled in the refrigerator for several days. Bake and serve oven-warm for a last-minute treat.

1 cup all-purpose flour
½ teaspoon salt
½ cup butter or margarine
1 cup leftover mashed potatoes
1 egg yolk
1 teaspoon milk
Fresh coarse ground pepper
Grated Parmesan cheese
Nonstick spray coating

In medium bowl, mix flour and salt. With a pastry blender or fork, blend butter thoroughly into flour. Stir in mashed potatoes until well mixed. Roll into a ball and place in a small bowl. Cover and refrigerate at least one hour to chill. Spray 2 baking sheets with nonstick spray coating and set aside. Preheat oven to 375°. On a lightly floured surface with floured rolling pin, roll out one-half of the potato dough until it's about ⅛-inch thick. (Dough will be fairly soft.) Keep second half in refrigerator until you are ready to roll it out. Cut dough into 3" x ½" strips. In a small cup, stir together egg yolk and milk. Brush the top of the strip with the mixture. Sprinkle with pepper and Parmesan cheese. Arrange strips on baking sheets. Bake for 20 minutes or until crisp and golden.

Makes about 4 dozen appetizers.

Note
Although the muffins look and taste great as is, you may want to garnish them with a sprinkle of sugar and cinnamon. Simply combine 1 tablespoon sugar and ½ teaspoon cinnamon over each unbaked muffin.

dilled potato scones

The potato cakes that so many cooks make with leftover mashed potatoes are, in reality, potato scones. Because they contain more potatoes than flour they are similar to a cross between potato cakes and baked scones. They offer a quick and easy way to use yesterday's mashed potatoes and make a tasty addition to any meal—morning, noon, or night.

1 cup all-purpose flour
¼ teaspoon baking powder
2 ½ cups seasoned mashed potatoes
2 tablespoons butter, melted
1 tablespoon dried dillweed
¾ teaspoon salt
¼ teaspoon pepper
¼ teaspoon nutmeg
2 eggs, beaten
Olive oil or butter for frying

In a small mixing bowl, stir together flour and baking powder and set aside. In a large mixing bowl, stir together potatoes, butter, dill, salt, pepper and nutmeg. Add eggs and flour mixture and mix well. Cover and chill in refrigerator for 1 hour. Turn dough out onto a lightly floured surface. Divide dough in half and pat half into ½-inch thick round. Cut in quarters to form 4 wedges. Repeat with remaining dough. If preparing ahead, place scones on wax paper-lined plate or baking sheet and refrigerate until ready to cook. In a large nonstick skillet or griddle, heat 1 tablespoon oil over medium-high heat. Cook scones, in batches if necessary, adding more oil as needed, for 5 minutes or until crusted and golden brown on both sides and heated through. Serve at once.

Makes 8 scones.

Tasty Variations

Vary the flavor of the potato scones by replacing the dillweed with these alternatives,
or combinations of:

- Minced onion
- Minced green or red peppers
- Snipped parsley or chives
- Grated Parmesan or other tasty cheese
- Diced ham
- Diced mushrooms
- 1 cup cooked and diced chicken
- Bacon, fried and crumbled

Note
Scones will keep for several days if tightly wrapped and refrigerated. They may be reheated in the microwave or spread with a little softened butter and heated in a 350° oven.

cocoa-spudnuts

There once was a Spudnut shop in downtown Appleton, Wisconsin. They sold the most delicious doughnuts. This recipe reminds me of the treats we found there. They are best served fresh.

3 potatoes, peeled and quartered
2 packages active dry yeast
1½ cups milk
½ cup vegetable oil
½ cup sugar
1½ teaspoons salt
2 eggs
7-7½ cups all-purpose flour
½ cup cocoa
1 teaspoon ground cinnamon
Oil for deep fat frying
Powdered sugar for dusting (optional)
Glaze* (optional)
Nonstick spray coating

In a small saucepan, cook potatoes covered with water until tender. Drain, reserving ½ cup of liquid in a large mixer bowl and cool to 110-115°. Dissolve yeast in potato liquid. Mash potatoes. Add potatoes, milk, oil, sugar, salt, and eggs. Beat with an electric mixer at medium speed until smooth. Combine flour with cocoa and cinnamon.

With a wooden spoon, add enough flour to the potato mixture to form a soft dough. Spray a bowl with nonstick spray coating. Place dough in prepared bowl, turning once to coat surface. Cover and let rise in a warm place until double in size, for about 1 hour. Punch dough down and let rise again, about 30 minutes. Turn out on lightly floured surface and roll to ½-inch thickness. Cut with a floured 3-inch doughnut cutter. In an electric skillet or deep-fat fryer, heat oil to 375°. Fry a few doughnuts at a time until golden brown on both sides. Remove with slotted spoon and drain on absorbent paper. If desired, coat doughnuts with powdered sugar or drop warm doughnuts into prepared glaze. Place on cooling rack until glaze is set.

Makes 4 dozen.

*chocolate glaze

4 cups confectioner's sugar
3 tablespoons cocoa
⅓ cup water
1 teaspoon vanilla

In a flat bowl combine ingredients until well mixed. Dip warm doughnuts in glaze.

spicy sweet potato prune bread

Cool this bread for several hours or overnight before slicing. If in a hurry, partly freeze bread and it will slice without crumbling.

Nonstick spray coating
1½ cups cooked and mashed
   sweet potatoes
1¼ cups sugar
⅓ cup cooking oil
2 eggs
1¾ cups all-purpose flour
2 teaspoons baking powder
¾ teaspoon salt
½ teaspoon cinnamon
¼ teaspoon ground cloves
¼ teaspoon ground ginger
1 cup pitted and snipped prunes*
½ cup chopped pecans

Preheat oven to 350°. Spray and lightly flour 9" x 5" loaf pan with nonstick spray coating. Set aside. In a large mixing bowl, combine sweet potatoes, sugar, oil and eggs; beat until smooth. In a small mixing bowl, combine flour, baking powder, salt, cinnamon, cloves and ginger. Add prunes and nuts; stir to coat. Slowly add dry ingredients to sweet potato mixture. Stir just until moistened. Spoon batter into prepared loaf pan. Bake for 1½ hours or until golden and toothpick inserted near the center comes out clean. Cool for 30 minutes on a wire rack.

Makes 1 loaf.

homemade croutons

Croutons are simple and quick to make. They are especially tasty when made with potato bread. Start with the following simple recipe or experiment with your favorite spice blends for a variety of interesting flavored croutons.

2 cups cubed day old potato bread,
   sourdough bread or rye bread
2 tablespoons butter or margarine, melted
¾ teaspoon of your favorite seasoning
   blend such as:
   Italian Herb seasoning
   Roasted Garlic seasoning
   Cheese or onion based seasonings

Preheat oven to 400°. Spread bread cubes in a single layer in a shallow baking dish. Stir together melted butter or margarine and seasoning. Pour over the bread cubes. Bake for 5 minutes. Stir and bake 5 to 10 minutes longer or until crisp and brown.

Makes 2 cups.

*Raisins or dates may be used in place of prunes.

rhubarb custard potato küchen

Mashed potatoes give this küchen base a velvety, cake-like texture, making it a perfect complement for the rhubarb custard. For a special treat, serve it warm from the oven with a dollop of sweetened whipped cream or a scoop of vanilla ice cream.

1 pound fresh rhubarb, trimmed, rinsed,
    and cut into ½-inch pieces
Water

For Küchen

2 ½ cups all-purpose flour
¼ cup sugar
½ teaspoon salt
1 teaspoon baking powder
1 cup butter or margarine
⅔ cup mashed potatoes
1 egg yolk
¼ cup milk
1 teaspoon vanilla

For Custard Topping

1 egg white
2 eggs
¾ cup sugar
¼ teaspoon salt
¼ cup milk
1 teaspoon vanilla
1 teaspoon ground nutmeg
Sweetened whipped cream for topping, if desired

Preheat oven to 350°. In a saucepan, using only sufficient water to start the cooking, cook the rhubarb for 10 minutes or until it is just tender. Remove from heat and allow to cool slightly. In a large mixing bowl combine flour, sugar, salt and baking powder. Add the butter and blend with a pastry blender or fork until mixture resembles fine crumbs. Add the mashed potatoes and egg yolk and continue blending until well mixed. Add milk and vanilla and moisten like a piecrust. Pat evenly into an ungreased 11" x 15" baking pan (a jelly roll pan works fine), being careful to create a slight edge all around. Pour 2 ½ cups cooked rhubarb over the top. Spread to the edges.

desserts

Desserts and potatoes make a great combination. Potatoes are the secret ingredient to many a sweet satisfaction. The versatile tuber lends its delectable flavor and moisture to a surprising array of luscious cakes, bars, pies and other goodies.

For the custard

In a small mixing bowl, beat together egg white, eggs, sugar, salt, milk and vanilla. Pour over the rhubarb. Sprinkle nutmeg lightly over the custard topping. Bake in preheated oven for 45 minutes or until knife inserted in custard topping comes out clean. Serve warm topped with sweetened whipped cream if desired.

Makes 10 to 12 servings.

Tasty Variation

Prepare rhubarb as directed. When cool, add 1 cup drained, crushed pineapple to the rhubarb. Continue as directed.

potato pecan torte

This easy-to-make, nut-laden torte will please everyone. For variety, use your favorite seasonal fruit or combination for garnish.

2 medium Russet potatoes, unpeeled
Nonstick spray coating
4 eggs, separated
1 cup plus 5 teaspoons sugar, divided
1 cup all-purpose flour
1 cup pecans, finely chopped
2 teaspoons grated orange rind
¾ teaspoon salt
½ teaspoon baking soda
1½ cups whipping cream
5 teaspoons cocoa
1 tablespoon finely crushed pecans,
   for garnish
1 cup large fresh raspberries, for garnish

In a medium saucepan, cook potatoes in water to cover until tender. Drain, peel, and rice potatoes. Preheat oven to 325°. Spray a 9" x 3" spring form pan with nonstick spray coating and lightly flour. Set aside. In a large mixing bowl, beat egg whites at high speed until soft peaks form. Gradually beat in ¼ cup sugar. Continue until whites stand in stiff glossy peaks. Set aside. In a small mixer bowl, beat egg yolks and ¾ cup sugar at medium speed until thick and light lemon colored. Scrape bowl occasionally. Add potatoes and continue beating until mixture is smooth. Stir in flour, pecans, orange rind, salt and baking soda until moistened. With a rubber spatula, fold egg-yolk mixture into egg-white mixture. Spread batter into prepared spring form pan. Bake in preheated oven for 1 hour or until torte springs back when lightly touched with finger. Cool torte completely in pan on a wire rack. In a small mixing bowl, beat whipping cream, 5 teaspoons of sugar, and 4½ teaspoons cocoa until soft peaks form. Remove torte from pan. Spread whipped cream on top and sides. Sprinkle with remaining cocoa and crushed pecans. Refrigerate until serving time. Arrange raspberries on top and around the bottom edge before serving.

Makes about 12 servings.

potato 'n apple spice cake

This is a delicious dessert served with whipped cream or ice cream.

Nonstick spray coating
½ cup butter or margarine
1 cup sugar
2 eggs, slightly beaten
⅔ cup unseasoned riced potatoes
1 cup all-purpose flour
1 teaspoon baking soda
¾ teaspoon salt
½ teaspoon cinnamon
½ teaspoon nutmeg
¼ teaspoon allspice
3 cups diced apples
¼ cup chopped walnuts
1 teaspoon vanilla
Whipped cream or ice cream (optional)

Preheat oven to 350°. Spray an 8" square cake pan with nonstick spray coating and lightly flour. In a large mixing bowl, combine butter, sugar, and eggs. Cream until light and fluffy. Blend in potatoes. In a small bowl, combine flour, baking soda, salt, cinnamon, nutmeg, and allspice. Fold into butter mixture, blending until well mixed. Fold in apples, nuts, and vanilla. Pour batter into prepared pan. Bake in preheated oven for 45 to 50 minutes or until wooden toothpick inserted near center comes out clean. Serve warm or cold, with or without whipped cream or ice cream.

Makes about 8 servings.

potato chip cookies

These chewy cookies have a secret ingredient that will have your family guessing. Be sure to use plain potato chips the first time you make them or omit the extra salt if you use salted potato chips.

1 cup granulated sugar
1 cup packed brown sugar
1 cup shortening
2 eggs, slightly beaten
1 teaspoon vanilla
2 cups all-purpose flour
1 teaspoon baking soda
¼ teaspoon salt
1 package (6-ounces)
  semi-sweet chocolate pieces
1 cup chopped nuts
2 cups crushed potato chips

Preheat oven to 350°. In a large mixing bowl, cream sugars and shortening until light and fluffy. Beat in eggs and vanilla. Add flour, baking soda, and salt. Stir in chocolate pieces, nuts, and chips. Stir only until well mixed. Drop by rounded teaspoons onto ungreased cookie sheet, placing them 2 inches apart. Lightly flatten with a fork. Bake for 10 to 12 minutes or until lightly browned and set. Remove from oven and cool on cookie sheets for 5 minutes, then remove to racks to finish cooling.

Makes about 5 dozen.

double chocolate potato drops

Potatoes and buttermilk combine to give these cake-like cookies a rich flavor and moist texture. They are attractive with a simple dusting of powdered sugar.

Nonstick spray coating
1½ cups all-purpose flour
½ teaspoon salt
½ teaspoon baking soda
½ cup butter or margarine
1 cup packed brown sugar
1 egg
1 teaspoon vanilla
½ cup mashed potatoes
2 envelopes (1 ounce each) premelted, unsweetened chocolate
¾ cup buttermilk
1 cup miniature semi-sweet chocolate pieces
½ cup chopped walnuts
¼ cup powdered sugar, for garnish

Preheat oven to 400°. Lightly spray a cookie sheet with nonstick spray coating. In medium mixing bowl, combine flour, salt, and baking soda. In a large mixing bowl, beat butter or margarine and brown sugar on medium-high speed until light and fluffy. Beat in egg and vanilla until well mixed. Add mashed potatoes and chocolate and continue beating until smooth. With a wooden spoon, stir in flour mixture alternately with buttermilk, stirring just until combined. Blend in chocolate pieces and walnuts. Drop dough by rounded teaspoons, 2 inches apart on prepared baking sheet. Bake for 8 to 10 minutes or until cookies spring back when touched by a finger. Do not over-bake. Leave cookies on baking sheets for a minute or two before removing to cool on rack. Dust cooled cookies with a sprinkling of powdered sugar.

Makes about 4 dozen cookies.

potato date bars

Easy to make, these bars will please everyone, especially the lunchbox and after-school crowd. This recipe produces a very moist bar. Make sure you carefully follow the baking time.

Nonstick spray coating
1 cup orange juice
1 cup dates, pitted and diced
1 teaspoon baking soda
½ cup butter
1¼ cup sugar
2 eggs
1 teaspoon vanilla
1¾ cup all-purpose flour
3 tablespoons cocoa
¼ teaspoon salt
1 cup mashed potatoes
½ cup pecans, chopped
½ cup mini chocolate chips

Preheat oven to 350°. Spray a 9" x 13" baking pan with nonstick spray coating. Lightly flour and set aside. In a small saucepan, bring orange juice to boil. Pour boiling orange juice over dates. Cool. Stir in baking soda and set aside. In a medium mixing bowl, cream butter and sugar together until light and fluffy. Beat in eggs, one at a time, and vanilla. In a small bowl, combine flour, cocoa, and salt. Add to butter mixture alternately with cooled date mixture, starting and ending with flour mixture. Add potatoes and beat for 5 minutes at medium-high speed, pausing occasionally to scrape down side of bowl. Pour batter into prepared pan. Sprinkle with pecans and chips. Bake for 45-50 minutes. Remove from oven and cool on wire rack.

Makes about 15 bars.

Variation

These bars can be served warm as a cake with a scoop of vanilla ice cream.

Makes about 15 servings.

One Potato, two potato, three Potato, four. Five potato, six potato, seven potato, more.

This simple chant has long been used by schoolchildren as a choosing rhyme.

potato-cranberry-apple crisp

The tart, tempting taste of red cranberries perfectly contrasts with the potatoes and apples in this all-time favorite family dessert.

Nonstick spray coating
1 cup shredded raw potatoes
2 cups fresh or frozen cranberries,
   coarsely chopped (one 12-ounce package)
3 cups coarsely chopped, peeled apples
1 cup granulated sugar
1½ cups rolled oats
1 cup, firmly packed, brown sugar
½ cup butter or margarine
¼ cup all-purpose flour
½ teaspoon salt
Cream or ice cream (optional)

Preheat oven to 375°. Spray a 9" pie pan or square cake pan with nonstick spray coating. In a mixing bowl combine potatoes, cranberries, apples, and granulated sugar. Mix well. Turn into prepared pan. In a small mixing bowl, combine oats, brown sugar, butter, flour, and salt. Mix with a pastry blender or fingertips until crumbly. Sprinkle over fruit. Bake in preheated oven for 1 hour or until cranberries and apples are tender and the top is lightly browned. Serve warm with cream or ice cream, if desired.

Makes about 6 servings.

orange fluff potato pie

This is an unusual recipe that makes a surprisingly good pie; surprising, because one doesn't expect to find a dessert pie made with mashed potatoes.

½ cup frozen orange juice concentrate
1 tablespoon fresh lemon juice
1 cup mashed potatoes
40 large marshmallows
1 (8-ounce) carton mandarin orange yogurt
1 cup whipping cream
Graham cracker crust for 9" pie
   (recipe on page 83)
¼ cup coconut, toasted*
1 (11-ounce) can mandarin orange sections,
   drained, for garnish

In a large microwave-safe mixing bowl, combine orange juice concentrate, lemon juice, and mashed potatoes. Stir in marshmallows. Microwave, covered, on high for 2½ to 3 minutes or until marshmallows are melted, stirring halfway through heating time. Pour mixture into blender or food processor. Blend until super smooth. Cool to room temperature. Stir in yogurt. In a small bowl, beat whipping cream until soft peaks form. Fold into marshmallow mixture. Pour pie filling into chilled graham cracker crust. Garnish with toasted coconut and mandarin orange sections. Cover and chill for 8 to 24 hours.

Makes one 9" pie.

*To toast coconut: Preheat oven to 350°. Spread coconut in a thin layer in a shallow baking pan. Bake for 5 to 10 minutes or until light golden brown, stirring once or twice.

mashed potato cheesecake

I'm confident you'll agree that this potato cheesecake makes a delicious dessert, especially when topped with fresh crushed, sweetened strawberries.

2 medium russet potatoes,
    peeled and cubed
1 cup water
1 tablespoon lemon juice
2 teaspoons grated lemon peel
¼ teaspoon salt
1¼ cups graham cracker crumbs
¼ cup butter or margarine, melted
3 (8-ounce) packages light cream cheese
1 cup sugar
4 eggs
1 (8-ounce) carton whipping cream
2 tablespoons powdered sugar, sifted
Fresh strawberries, crushed and sweetened
    to taste (optional)

Preheat oven to 350°. In a small saucepan with water, boil potatoes, covered, until very tender. Do not drain. Mash until very smooth or place mixture in blender and blend until smooth. Measure mixture; discard some or add water as necessary to make 1¾ cups total. Stir in lemon juice, lemon peel, and salt. Set aside. In a bowl, combine graham cracker crumbs and melted butter; toss to mix well. Spread in an even layer in a 9" spring form pan or a 9" x 9" x 2" baking pan. Bake in preheated oven for 10 minutes. Meanwhile, in a large mixing bowl, beat cream cheese and sugar until fluffy. Beat in potato mixture until well blended. Add eggs all at once and beat until just mixed. Do not overbeat. Pour into crust-lined pan. Bake at 325° for about 1 hour or just until set in center. Remove to a rack to cool. With a sharp knife, loosen cheesecake from sides of pan before cooling to help prevent excess cracking. Chill. To serve, beat whipping cream and powdered sugar until soft peaks form. Spread on top of cheesecake, topping with fresh strawberries if desired.

Makes 12 to 16 servings.

spicy sweet potato pie

Famous old-fashioned sweet potato pie with a touch of orange flavor and a pecan crust: The perfect ending to a special dinner.

Pecan pastry for 9" single crust pie (recipe on page 83)
2 medium sweet potatoes
2 eggs
1⅔ cups evaporated milk
¾ cup sugar
1 tablespoon grated orange peel
1 tablespoon triple sec
½ teaspoon salt
1 teaspoon ground cinnamon
½ teaspoon ground ginger
¼ teaspoon ground nutmeg
1 cup whipping cream
2 tablespoons triple sec or orange juice
1 teaspoon sugar
Orange zest for garnish (optional)

Wash and cook sweet potatoes in boiling water to cover until fork tender. Drain. Cool and mash. Measure out 2 cups of mashed sweet potatoes. Meanwhile, preheat oven to 425°. In a large mixing bowl, beat eggs slightly. Add sweet potatoes, milk, sugar, orange peel, triple sec, salt, cinnamon, ginger, and nutmeg. Beat on low until well blended. Pour into pastry-lined pie pan. Bake in preheated oven for 15 minutes. Reduce oven temperature to 350°. Continue to bake for another 45 minutes or until knife inserted near center comes out clean. Remove from oven and cool on a wire rack. In a chilled bowl, beat whipping cream until stiff. In last minute of beating, add 2 tablespoons of triple sec and the remaining teaspoon of sugar. Cut pie into serving slices and add a generous dollop of whipped cream to each. Circle orange zest across the whipped cream.

Makes one 9" pie.

Tips

- Cook the sweet potatoes in their jackets to allow the natural sugars just under the skins to carmelize for a delicious flavor.

- To prevent spills on the way to the oven, place pie plate on oven rack while filling with the Sweet Potato mixture.

graham cracker crust

4 tablespoons butter or margarine
2 tablespoons sugar
2 teaspoons finely shredded orange peel
1 1/4 cups finely crushed graham crackers

Preheat oven to 375°. Melt butter. Mix in
sugar and shredded orange peel. Stir in
crushed graham crackers. Pour mixture
into a 9" pie plate. Press onto bottom and
sides to form a firm, even crust. Bake for 6
to 8 minutes or until edges are lightly
browned. Chill crust for at least 30
minutes before filling.

pecan pastry
for 9" single crust pie

1 1/2 cups all-purpose flour
1/2 teaspoon salt
1/2 cup shortening
1/4 cup finely crushed pecans
4-5 tablespoons cold water

In a medium bowl, combine flour and salt.
Cut in shortening until pieces are the size of
small peas. Stir in crushed pecans. Sprinkle
in water, 1 tablespoon at a time, tossing the
mixture after each addition, until all flour is
moistened and pastry almost cleans sides of
bowl. Add more water if needed. Form into a
ball. Place dough on lightly floured surface.
Flatten dough with hands. Using a lightly
floured rolling pin, roll dough out from center
to edges, forming a circle about 12 inches in
diameter. Wrap pastry about rolling pin.
Unroll onto a 9" pie plate. Ease pastry into
pie plate, being careful not to stretch pastry.
Trim overhanging edge of pastry 1 inch from
rim of pan. Fold and roll pastry under, even
with pan flute. Do not prick pastry. Follow
baking directions in the previous recipes.

crunchy ice cream balls

A simple make-ahead dessert that's sure to please both family and dinner guests.

2 cups crushed ripple potato chips
1 cup flaked sweetened coconut
1 teaspoon cinnamon
2 pints vanilla ice cream
½ cup maple syrup
Whipped cream
Maraschino cherries

Preheat oven to 325°. In a large flat baking pan (jelly roll type), combine crushed potato chips, coconut and cinnamon. Bake in preheated oven for 10 minutes or until coconut is toasted golden. Cool. Shape ice cream into balls. Roll ice cream balls in the chip mixture, making sure the mixture is pressed firmly into the ice cream. Freeze. When ready to serve, place the ice cream balls in a serving dish and drizzle with maple syrup. Top with whipped cream and a maraschino cherry.

Makes about 8 servings.

Variations

- Your favorite ice cream flavor may be substituted for the vanilla ice cream in this recipe.

- Honey may be substituted for the maple syrup.

chocolate-dipped chips

Here is a quick, sweet treat that will appeal to kids of all ages.

3 (6-ounce) packages chocolate-flavored almond bark
1 (14-ounce) package of ridged potato chips

In a small bowl, melt chocolate bark in microwave. Dip tip of chip in the warm chocolate. Handle carefully so chips don't break. Place on a large ungreased cookie sheet to cool. Let set until chocolate hardens.

coconut potato candy bites

This chocolate-covered coconut potato candy is as tempting as a candy bar.

¾ cup diced potato
Nonstick spray coating
4 cups powdered sugar
4 cups flaked sweetened coconut
1 teaspoon almond extract
½ teaspoon salt
4 ounces unsweetened chocolate
¼ cup crushed walnuts

In a small saucepan, cook the potato in boiling water until tender. Drain. Mash well and let cool. Meanwhile, spray a 9" x 13" pan with nonstick spray coating. In a large mixing bowl, mix the potato with the powdered sugar. Stir in the coconut, almond extract and salt. Mix well. Press the mixture into the prepared pan. In a double boiler, melt the chocolate over hot water (do not let the water boil). Pour and spread the chocolate over the candy. Sprinkle crushed walnuts over the warm chocolate. Let cool. To serve cut into small squares.

Makes about 2 ½ pounds.

Fresh Potato Types and Their Preparation

Following is a basic overview of the main types of potatoes and their culinary uses and preparation.

- Russet
- Round White
- Long White
- Round Red
- Yellow Flesh
- Blue and Purple

Russet Potatoes

This is the most widely used potato variety in the United States. A large majority is grown in the Northwest. They are available year-round. These potatoes are high in starch and are characterized by netted brown skin and white flesh. Russets are light and fluffy when cooked, making them ideal for baking and mashing. They are also wonderful for frying and roasting.

Round White Potatoes

These are grown and used most often in the Eastern United States. They are available year-round. Round whites are medium in starch level and have smooth, light tan skin with white flesh. These are creamy in texture and hold their shape well after cooking. Regarded an all-purpose potato, round whites are very versatile and can be used in most potato preparations.

Long White Potatoes

These are grown primarily in California and are available spring through summer. Long whites are oval-shaped, medium in starch level and have thin, light tan skin. They have a firm, creamy texture when cooked. These all-purpose potatoes are very versatile and can be used in most potato preparations.

Round Red Potatoes

These potatoes are available mostly in late summer and early fall. They are characterized by their rosy red skin and white flesh. Red potatoes have a firm, smooth and moist texture, making them well suited for salads, roasting, boiling and steaming. Round reds are often referred to as "new potatoes"; however, technically, "new" refers to any variety of potatoes that is harvested before reaching maturity.

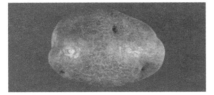

Yellow Flesh Potatoes

These potatoes are very popular in Europe and increasingly popular in the United States, although they are still not grown in large quantities. Yellow flesh potatoes are available in late summer and early fall. These potatoes have a dense, creamy texture. With their golden color, you can be fooled into thinking that they are buttered.

Blue and Purple Potatoes

Photo courtesy Potato Section, Plant Health and Production Division, Canadian Food Inspection Agency.

These potatoes originated in South America and are not widely cultivated in the United States. Blue and purple potatoes are most available in the fall. These relatively uncommon tubers have a subtle nutty flavor and flesh that ranges in hue from dark blue or lavender to white. Microwaving preserves the color best, but steaming and baking are also favorable methods of preparation.

North American Potato Varieties

The following is an alphabetical listing of the recognized
strains of potatoes in North America. These varieties fall
within the six main categories covered in the previous section.

Variety Name	Characteristics
Allegany	Very late season variety grown primarily for table use and commercial potato chip processing. Round shape with buff skin color and texture ranging from smooth to slightly netted, and shallow eyes. White flesh. Has long storage life.

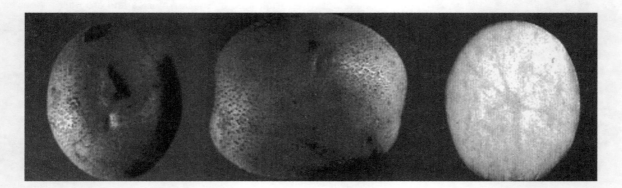

Atlantic Oval to round shape with light-to-heavy scaly netted medium brown skin. Moderately shallow eyes and white flesh. Primarily grown to make potato chips.

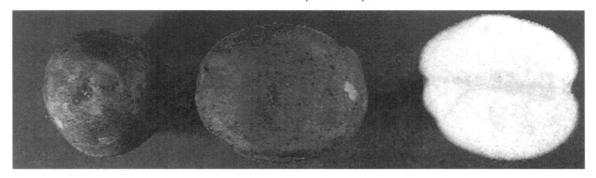

Belrus Long, slightly flattened shape of uniform consistency with shallow, well-distributed eyes. Heavily russeted skin with cream-colored flesh. Medium storage capacity. Exceptional for baking and French frying.

Calwhite Oblong, light-skinned with shallow eyes in
moderate abundance. Short storage life.
Very large potatoes are versatile in the kitchen
and commercial frozen food processing.

Cascade Oblong with shallow eyes on bright, light smooth
skin that may show occasionally slight cracks.
A main season variety initially grown for
commercial French fry production, it now
serves as a versatile kitchen potato.

Castile Oblong, slightly flattened shape with shallow eyes on smooth, light skin. White flesh is adaptable to a wide range of preparation methods. A good overall potato.

Centennial Russet Oblong shape, blocky and slightly flattened with smooth, thick, dark netted brown skin. Shallow eyes and white flesh.

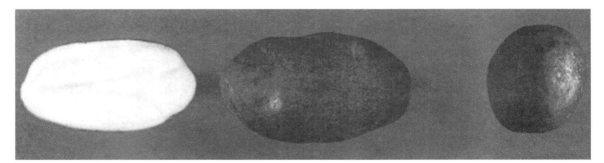

Century Russet Long, cylindrical tubers, slightly flattened with lightly and uniformly russeted skin. Medium-shallow eyes with a distinct "eyebrow" are moderate in number and evenly distributed. White flesh has high sugar content. Medium storage qualities with broad kitchen versatility.

Chieftain Oblong to round, medium-thick shape with smooth, medium red skin and white flesh. Shallow, well-distributed eyes with medium storage life. An especially attractive potato, adaptable to most uses except frying. Displays a tendency toward skinning.

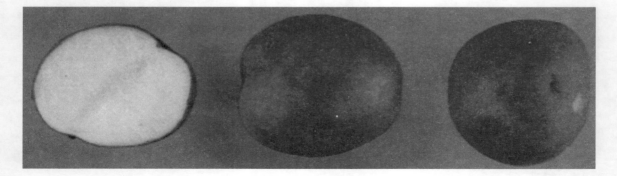

Chipeta Primarily grown for commercial chip processing, a late season variety of large size with round to oval shape, light skin and white flesh. Skin is commonly covered with small, russeted areas and moderately deep eyes. Medium storage life.

Frontier Russet Oblong to long cylindrical shape with blocky ends and medium to light russet skin. White flesh suited for baking and French frying.

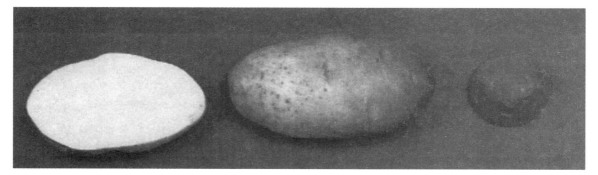

Gemchip Mid-to-late season variety with round to short oblong shape. Smooth, light skin may have small scaly patches, and the bud end has a shallow to moderately deep indent. Versatile, mainly grown for commercial chip production.

Goldrush Mid-season variety grown primarily for the fresh market. Oblong, blocky shape of average to exceptional length. Medium brown skin with shallow, well-distributed eyes that may show a reddish blush. Very white flesh with medium storage life. Attractive texture and flavor.

Hilite Russet Smooth, oblong to long shape with medium to heavy russet skin. Unusually free of any defects and uniform size. Good baking and frying qualities.

Irish Cobbler An early season variety with very good eating quality. Round, medium to large in size with shallow to deep eyes on creamy light, smooth skin. White flesh.

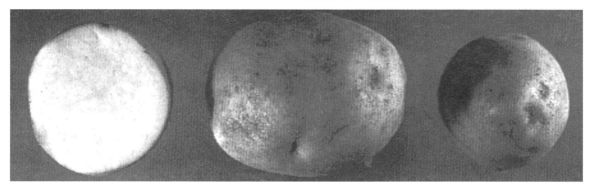

Itasca Mid-season variety with round or blocky shape and smooth, light skin with shallow eyes. Larger potatoes will have longer shapes. White flesh. Stores well.

Kanona Mid-season variety grown mostly for commercial chip producers. Large tubers tending toward round or oval shape with light, slightly netted skin and medium-deep eyes. Creamy-colored flesh has good cooking quality.

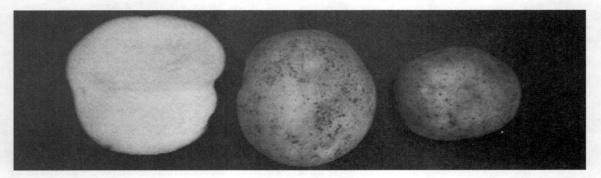

Katahdin A common table use variety. Round to oblong with buff, smooth skin and white flesh. Shallow to moderately deep eyes. Average cooking quality.

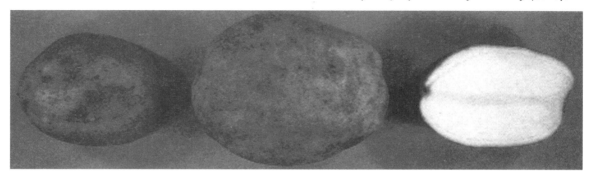

Kennebec Primarily used for commercial French fry production as well as table use. Oblong, slightly flat shape with shallow eyes. Has a tendency toward misshapen tubers, but this does not affect their taste or cooking quality. Thin, smooth light brown skin. Grows best in cool conditions, and has a moderate storage life. Good cooking quality.

Krantz Oblong to slightly blocky shape with lightly netted, russet skin and shallow eyes. White flesh has exceptional boiling and baking qualities. Makes great French fries.

La Chipper More elongated than round and somewhat flattened shape. Smooth, light skin with medium to deep, cream-colored eyes fairly evenly distributed. Very white flesh with relatively short storage life. Primarily grown for commercial potato chip processing. Deep eyes and irregular shapes make them difficult to work with in the kitchen.

La Rouge Medium size oblong, flattened and somewhat irregular shape. Smooth skin is bright red when harvested from green vines, but fades as tubers mature. Tendency toward skinning with moderately deep eyes, well-distributed. Medium white to cream-colored flesh. Good boiling characteristics. A late yield variety, La Rouge is a popular winter potato.

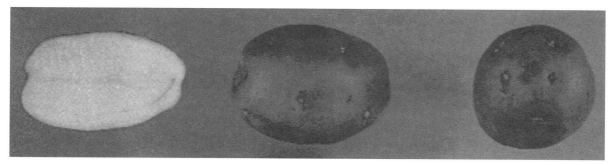

Lemhi Russet Oblong to long with rounded ends and a tannish-brown, medium to heavy netted skin and white flesh. Texture is excellent for baking and French fries.

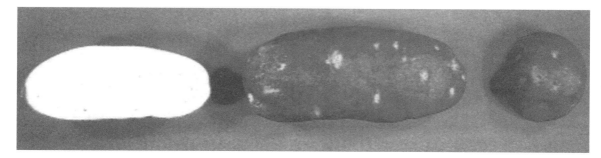

Monona Widely used to make potato chips. Oblong to oval, somewhat irregular flattened shape. Smooth, light buff skin with white flesh and shallow to medium-deep eyes. Stores well in longer-term cold storage, very good for table use.

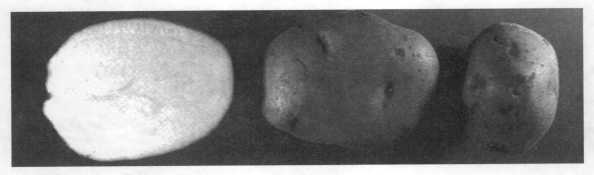

Nooksack Late-season stock with good appearance and excellent quality. Oblong to long and flattened shape with heavily russeted skin. Eyes are shallow, few and unevenly distributed. Exceptional storage quality.

Norchip Round to oblong shape with smooth, light skin. Mixture of shallow and deep eyes. White flesh. Grown for potato chips and table use.

Nordonna Mid-season variety that produces exceptionally consistent potatoes. Oval to round-oblong shape with shallow, well-distributed eyes on dark red skin. White flesh performs best when used fresh.

Norgold Russet Oblong to long shape is somewhat wider than thick. Uniformly netted, medium brown skin. White flesh is excellent for baking and boiling, but does not fry well.

Norking Russet A mid-season variety best used fresh. Oblong and blocky with medium to heavy russet skin. Shallow eyes display short, slightly curved "eyebrows." Long storage life and white flesh make it a good overall kitchen variety, especially good for frying.

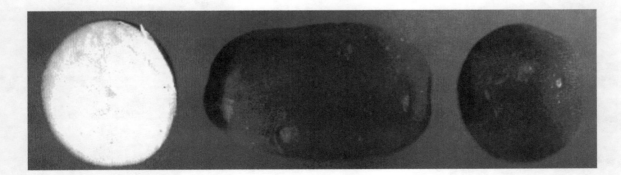

Norland Oblong, smooth and lightly flattened shape with a medium red skin and shallow eyes. Excellent for boiling and frying, fair for baking. Rarely misshapen or cracked.

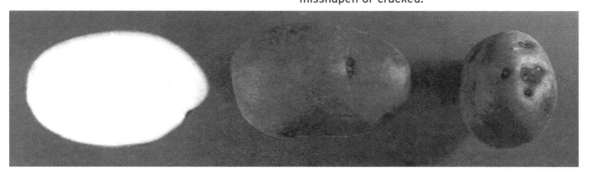

Norwis Mid-season variety shows blocky oval, slightly flattened shape and large size. Smooth light skin with relatively shallow eyes. Flesh is pale yellow to cream color. Not suited to long-term storage. Primarily grown for commercial chip makers.

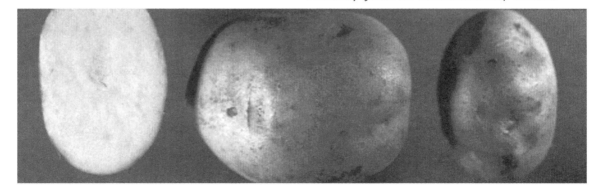

Onaway Early maturing variety makes it a popular fresh-from-the-field market potato. Short, rounded shape with smooth skin that flakes slightly when mature. Medium-deep eyes and white flesh. Has a tendency to produce misshapen tubers and does not store well.

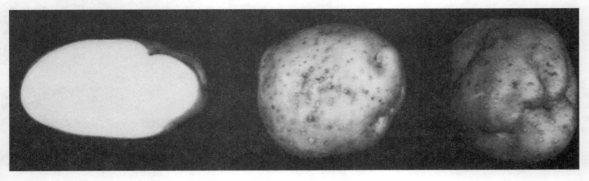

Ontario Oblong shape with creamy buff, smooth skin and shallow eyes. White flesh is susceptible to after-cooking darkening, especially when stored.

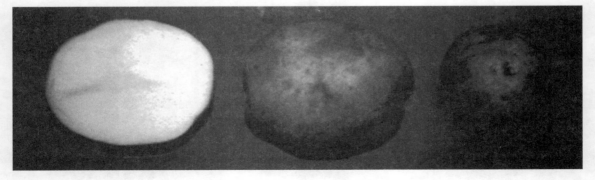

Pike Main season variety produces medium-sized, spherically shaped tubers with a mixture of shallow and moderately deep eyes. Used primarily for commercial chip processing, since a tendency toward after-cooking darkening and sloughing makes them unsuitable for table use.

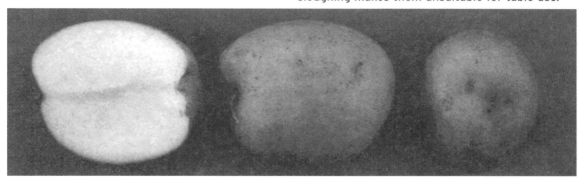

Ranger Russet A full-season variety with long, slightly flattened shape. Russet skin is tannish-brown and not scaly with plentiful, moderately shallow to deep, well-distributed eyes. Medium storage capacity. Versatile kitchen use.

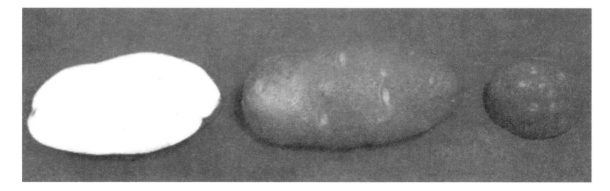

Red La Soda Round to oblong, slightly flattened shape with medium deep eyes. Smooth red skin has a tendency toward skinning. White flesh with long storage capacity and excellent for boiling. Popular in winter as a fresh market variety.

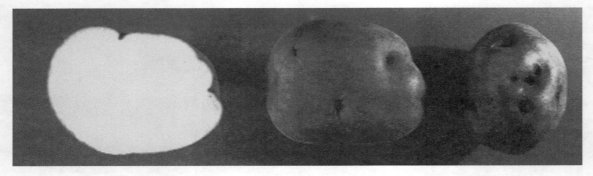

Red Pontiac Also called Dakota Chief. A late season variety with round to oblong tubers. Dark red skin may show netting. Medium deep eyes, white flesh and used mostly for fresh market and seed export. Medium to long storage properties. Resists darkening after cooking.

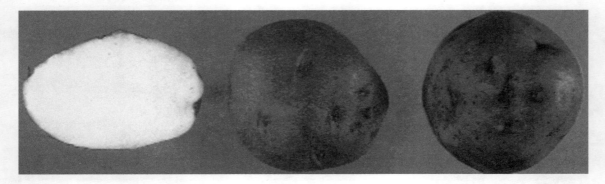

Red Ruby A good mid-season fresh market variety. Round to blocky in shape with dark red, smooth skin that shows occasional slight netting. Excellent, attractive color with white flesh

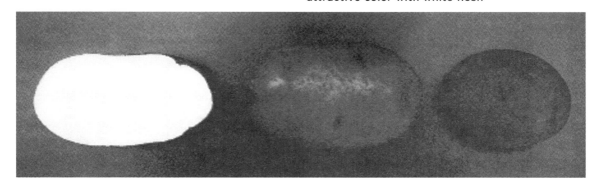

Russet Burbank A late-maturing variety with large, long cylindrical or slightly flattened shape. Russet skin with shallow eyes and white flesh. Usually uniform in shape, good long-term storage.

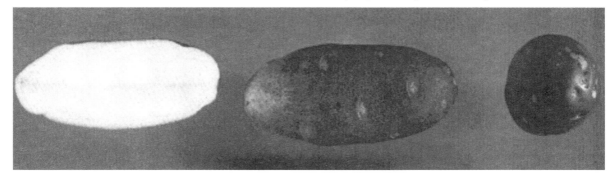

Russet Norkotah An early-to-mid-season variety popular with the fresh market. Long to oblong shape with smooth, russeted skin and shallow, bright golden eyes. White flesh with medium storage life. Attractive in appearance and good for general table use.

Russet Nugget Late-season potatoes with heavily and uniformly russeted skin and white flesh. Oblong, slightly flattened shape with shallow eyes moderate in number and well-distributed. White flesh has a high Vitamin C content and performs well in a variety of preparations.

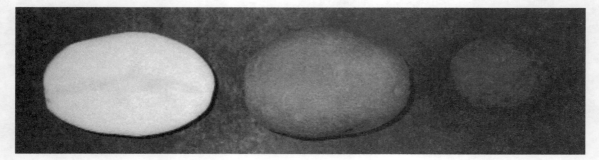

Sangre Mid-season, fresh market variety has oval to oblong shape. Smooth, dark red skin is slightly to moderately netted with shallow eyes. Excellent for boiling and baking.

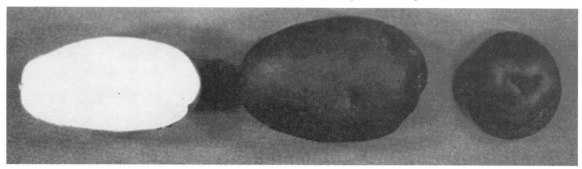

Sebago A late-season potato with elliptical to round shape of medium thickness. Smooth, very light skin with very shallow eyes make them perfect for peeling. Short storage life but versatile in use.

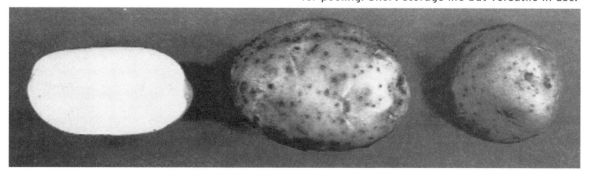

Shepody Primarily grown for commercial French fry processing. Oblong to long shape with smooth, lightly netted light skin and medium-deep eyes. White flesh with a relatively large and uniform size, excellent for frying.

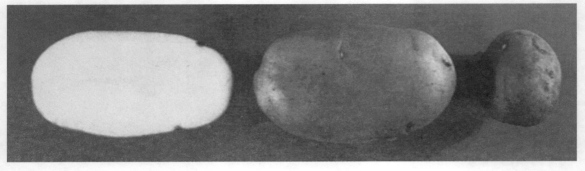

Snowden Full-season variety with round, slightly flattened shape and slightly netted, medium light skin. Medium eye depth. Produced mainly for commercial chip production.

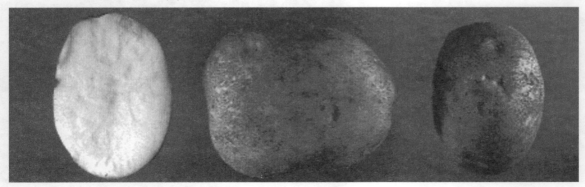

Superior A medium to early maturing variety with round to oblong shapes, slightly irregular with medium deep eyes and white flesh. Good storage capacity but sometimes pressure bruises in long-term.

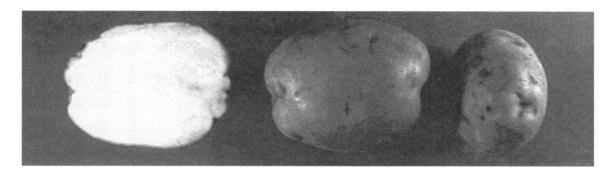

Viking Large, oblong to round shape with medium thickness. Smooth, medium-to-deep red skin with shallow, well-distributed eyes. Excellent for versatile culinary use.

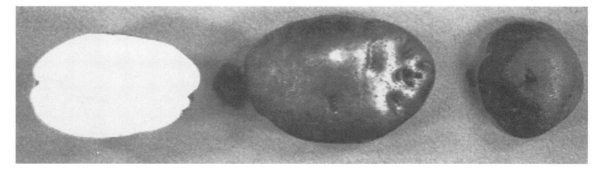

White Rose Also called American Giant, Wisconsin Pride, Late Pride, California Long White or Long White. Large, long, elliptical shape with slight flattening. Smooth white skin with deep eyes and white flesh. Available in early spring and summer, and excellent for boiling, mashing and baking.

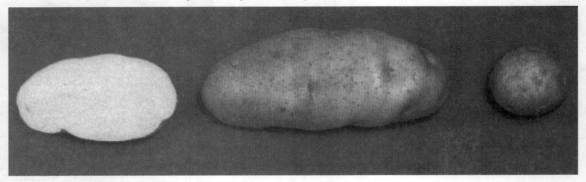

Yukon Gold Mid-to-late season variety with slightly oval and often somewhat flattened shape. Yellow-white skin with shallow, pink eyes and light yellow flesh. Flesh color is retained during baking, boiling or French frying. An attractive variety excellent for fresh market use.

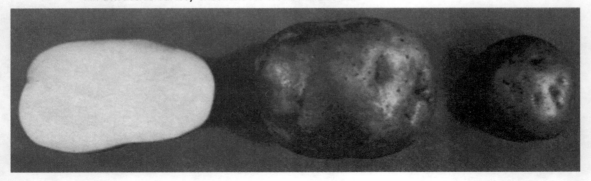

The Nutritional Value of Potatoes

Seventy to eighty percent of a potato's weight is water, making it a food that stores most of its nutrients in twenty to thirty percent of its bulk. That's a significant ratio of satisfaction to calories! Many people are misled about the fat content of potatoes, due to the high caloric value of many of the toppings people tend to put on their spuds.

Following is a breakdown of the potato's nutritional value as part of a sensible diet, based on a 100 gram potato.

Calories 84

Vitamins

B1 . . . . 0.10 mg

B2 . . . . 0.04 mg

B6 . . . . 0.20 mg

C . . . . 25 mg

Proteins . . . . 2 g

Fats 0.1g

Carbohydrates . . . . 19 g

Calcium . . . . 10 mg

Phosphorus . . . . 60 mg

Iron . . . . 0.5 mg

Sodium . . . . 14 mg

Potassium . . . . 600 mg

Weights and Measures

Equivalencies

The recipes in this book call for standard measuring
cups and spoons. A standard measuring cup equals ½ pint.
All measurements given are level. Eggs are large size.

3 teaspoons	=	1 tablespoon
1 rounded tablespoon	=	2 tablespoons
4 tablespoons	=	¼ cup
16 tablespoons	=	1 cup
1 cup	=	½ pint
2 cups	=	1 pint
2 pints	=	1 quart
4 quarts	=	1 gallon
8 quarts	=	1 peck
4 pecks	=	1 bushel
16 ounces	=	1 pound
16 liquid ounces	=	1 pint (2 cups)
5 eggs	=	about 1 cup
8 egg whites	=	about 1 cup
2 cups butter	=	1 pound
Butter the size of an egg	=	¼ cup
4 cups grated chesse	=	1 pound
3 medium sliced potatoes	=	1 pound
	=	2 cups mashed potatoes

Testing The Heat

Making French Fries

If you want to make French fries but don't have a deep fat thermometer, try this method to determine when your fat or oil is hot enough to start frying:

Heat the fat slowly. Drop a one-inch cube of day-old bread into it. When the cube browns in 20 seconds, your fat or oil is ready for your raw potato strips.

Oven Temperatures

At some time or other, you've probably heard of the following terms for how hot an oven you need to bake a particular item, but possibly didn't know exactly what was meant by seemingly arbitrary definitions. Chances are, you first heard the terms from a grandmother who learned to cook on a wood or coal stove without a built-in thermometer. Although each term does refer to a range of temperatures, they do indeed refer to a specific heat measurement. Temperatures are given in degrees Fahrenheit.

Very slow. . . . . 225-250°

Slow . . . . 250-300°

Moderate . . . . 300-350°

Moderately Hot . . . . 350-400°

Hot . . . . 400-450°

Very Hot . . . . 450-550°

General Preparation and Cooking Terms

Au Gratin Food (usually creamed) covered with bread crumbs and butter or cheese and baked until top is brown

Baste To moisten food being cooked with juices from pan or with additional liquid

Boil To cook in boiling water (212°F)

Braise To cook in a covered dish with a small amount of liquid

Broil Cooking at moderately hot temperature, turning several times

Brush To spread very thinly with brush or small paper or cloth

Cook until firm Until food is firm when touched with finger

Cook until tender Until fork can be easily inserted; in the case of vegetables and fruit, a straw may be used instead of a fork

Fricasee To combine pan frying and stewing methods

Fry To cook in deep fat or oil

Garnish To use one food to decorate another

Grill Same as broil

Marinate	To soak in any number of liquids, such as dressing, vinegar or lemon juice, before cooking
Mince	To chop very finely
Pan broil	To cook in a hot pan without grease
Parboil	To cook partly; not to complete cooking
Purée	Pulp and juice of a vegetable that has been rubbed through a sieve, ricer, blender or food processor
Roast	To bake something other than a dessert or bread item
Sauté or brown	Also called pan frying; to cook in small amount of fat or oil
Scald	To cover with boiling water
Sear	To form a coating on food quickly by heat
Shred	To cut into very thin slices
Simmer	To cook slowly, without boiling, with temperature just below the boiling point
Steam	To cook over, but not in, boiling water
Stew	To cook gently in small amount of liquid for an extended period

Common Ingredient Substitutions

In the preparation of some dishes in this book, you may find you've run out of a specific ingredient. Following is a list of acceptable substitutes for commonly used ingredients.

Ingredient	Measure	Substitution
Baking powder	1 teaspoon	¼ teaspoon baking soda plus ⅝ teaspoon cream of tartar
Bread crumbs, dry	¼ cup	1 slice bread
Bread crumbs, soft	½ cup	1 slice bread
Buttermilk	1 cup	1 cup plain yogurt
Cracker crumbs	¾ cup	1 cup dry bread crumbs
Cream, heavy	1 cup	¾ cup milk plus ⅓ cup melted butter (this mixture will not whip)
Cream, light	1 cup	⅞ cup milk plus 3 tablespoons melted butter
Cream, sour	1 cup	⅞ cup buttermilk or plain yogurt plus 3 tablespoons melted butter
Cream, whipping	1 cup	⅔ cup well-chilled evaporated milk, whipped; OR 1 cup nonfat dry milk powder whipped with 1 cup ice water

Ingredient	Measure	Substitution
Flour, all-purpose	1 cup	1⅛ cups cake flour; OR ⅝ cup potato flour; OR 1¼ cups rye four or coarsely ground whole-grain flour; OR 1 cup cornmeal
Flour, self-rising	1 cup	1 cup all-purpose flour plus 1¼ teaspoons baking powder plus ¼ teaspoon salt
Garlic	1 small clove	⅛ teaspoon garlic powder or instant minced garlic
Herbs, dried	½-1 teaspoon	1 tablespoon fresh herbs, minced and packed
Honey	1 cup	1¼ cups sugar plus ½ cup liquid
Lemon juice	1 teaspoon	½ teaspoon vinegar
Juice of 1 lemon	1 lemon	3 tablespoons bottled lemon or lime juice
Milk, skim	1 cup	⅓ cup instant nonfat dry milk plus ¾ cup water
Milk, to sour	1 cup	1 cup minus 1 tablespoon milk, plus 1 tablespoon vinegar or lemon juice. Stir and let stand 5 minutes.
Mustard, prepared	1 tablespoon	1 teaspoon dry or powdered mustard

Ingredient	Measure	Substitution
Onion, chopped	1 small	1 tablespoon instant minced onion; OR 1 teaspoon onion powder; OR ¾ cup chopped onion
Sugar, granulated	1 cup	1 cup firmly packed brown sugar; OR 1¾ cups confectioners' sugar (this won't work for baking); OR ½ cup honey; OR 1 cup superfine sugar; OR 1½ cups corn syrup; OR ⅔ cup maple syrup (for last two, reduce liquid in recipe by 25%)
Tomatoes, canned	1 cup	½ cup tomato sauce plus ½ cup water; OR 1⅓ cups chopped fresh tomatoes, simmered
Tomato juice	1 cup	½ cup tomato sauce plus ½ cup water plus dash each salt and sugar; OR ¼ cup tomato paste plus ¾ cup water plus salt and sugar to taste

references

colorado potato administrative committee
P.O. Box 348
Monte Vista, Colorado 81144
719-852-3322
www.coloradopotatoes.org

idaho potato commission
P.O. 1068 599 W Bannock
Boise, ID 83701
208 334-2350
www.idahopotato.com

maine potato board
744 Main Street Suite 1
Presque Isle, ME 04769
207 769-5061
www.mainepotatoes.com

the national potato promotion board
7555 E. Hampden Ave. #412
Denver, CO 80231
303-369-7783
www.potatohelp.com

the potato association of america
University of Maine
5715 Coburn Hall,
Room 6
Orono, ME 04469-5715
Phone: 207-581-3042
Fax: 207-581-3015
E-mail: umpotato@mail.maine.edu
www.ume.maine.edu/PAA

red river valley potato growers association
420 Business Highway 2
Box 301
East Grand Forks, MN 56721
218 773-3633
www.rrvpotatoes.org

washington state potato commission
108 Interlake Road
Moses Lake, WA 98837
509 765-8845
www.potatoes.com

wisconsin potato & vegetable growers association, inc.
P.O. Box 327
Antigo, WI 54409-0327
715 623-7683
www.potatowis.org

canadian food inspection agency
www.inspection.gc.ca
www.gc.ca

index

N

O

P

T

V

W

About the Author

Award-winning author Darlene Kronschnabel has been helping cooks please palates for more than twenty years through newspaper and magazine columns, articles, workshops and an extensive collection of cookbooks for such respected publishers as Better Homes and Gardens, Ideals, and Reiman Publications. Specializing in country style cooking and the particular dietary needs of diabetics, she has also edited a number of books, including a Spice and Herb Cookbook for the Durkee Company. Darlene is a member of the International Association of Culinary Professionals, the Culinary History Enthusiasts of Wisconsin, Wisconsin Regional Writers Association and the Council for Wisconsin Writers. The excellence of her work has been recognized with numerous awards from the Wisconsin Regional Writers Association, Wisconsin Press Women, the National Federation of Press Women and the Council for Wisconsin Writers.